CHASING
Heaven

What Dying Taught Me About Living

CRYSTAL MCVEA
and ALEX TRESNIOWSKI

HOWARD BOOKS
AN IMPRINT OF SIMON & SCHUSTER, INC.

New York   Nashville   London   Toronto   Sydney   New Delhi

Howard Books
An Imprint of Simon & Schuster, Inc.
1230 Avenue of the Americas
New York, NY 10020

Copyright © 2016 by Crystal McVea and Alex Tresniowski

Certain names and identifying characteristics have been changed.

First Howard Books hardcover edition March 2016

HOWARD and colophon are trademarks of Simon & Schuster, Inc.

For information about special discounts for bulk purchases, please contact Simon & Schuster Special Sales at 1-866-506-1949 or business@simonandschuster.com.

The Simon & Schuster Speakers Bureau can bring authors to your live event. For more information, or to book an event, contact the Simon & Schuster Speakers Bureau at 1-866-248-3049 or visit our website at www.simonspeakers.com.

Manufactured in the United States of America

10 9 8 7 6 5 4 3 2 1

Library of Congress Cataloging-in-Publication Data
Title: Chasing heaven : what dying taught me about living / by Crystal McVea
    with Alex Tresniowski.
Description: First [edition]. | Nashville : Howard, 2016.
Identifiers: LCCN 2015037133 | ISBN 9781501124938 (hardcover)
Subjects: LCSH: Heaven—Christianity—Miscellanea. | Near-death
        experiences—Religious aspects—Christianity. | Life—Religious aspects—
Christianity. | Christian life. | McVea, Crystal.
Classification: LCC BT848 .M375 2016 | DDC 248.4—dc23 LC record
available at http://lccn.loc.gov/2015037133

ISBN 978-1-5011-2491-4
ISBN 978-1-5011-2493-8 (ebook)

This book is dedicated in loving memory to James Wills, the greatest PawPaw a girl could ever have. And also to my dear sweet friend Wendy Cralley—it brings me great comfort to know that one day I will meet you both again at the gates of heaven.

Contents

Introduction

FIVE YEARS AFTER I DIED, I FOUND MYSELF STAND-ing on the filthy sidewalk of a desolate street in the worst part of town in the dead of night—on my way into a strip club.

"Hey, church ladies," an absolute giant of a man dressed in all black said to me and another woman as we stepped out of a van in front of the club. "What you got for me tonight?"

While he spoke to us, he ran a metal detector up and down the legs of the men waiting to get into the club, checking them for guns and knives.

I looked down at the small paper bag in my shaking hands. It was filled with cookies. With a plastered-on smile and my heart pounding in my chest, I offered the bag to him.

"Ohhh, chocolate chip," he said. "My favorite!"

Then he waved us inside.

As I walked through the front door, everything hit me all at once. The strong smell of smoke. The thumping, jarring music. The dollar bills and bottles of liquor on the tables. The men, young and old and in between, eager to spend their money. I swallowed hard.

This was no place I should ever have been.

I was a wife and a mother and a schoolteacher, and I lived in a small suburban town smack-dab in the middle of the country. Waiting for me back at home were my precious twins, Micah and Willow, not yet six years old. I also had two teenage children, who knew me as the woman who pestered them to clean up their rooms, not a woman who had to be searched for weapons by a bouncer.

So how in the world did I end up there?

I was there because, through tears of desperation one dark night, I called out to God.

"Break my heart for what breaks Yours," I cried.

And God did.

My name is Crystal McVea and on December 10, 2009, I died.

While I was being treated in a hospital for pancreatitis, I went into respiratory arrest. My heart stopped pumping and I stopped breathing for nine minutes while a team of doctors performed CPR and managed to revive me.

And in those nine minutes, I went to the gates of heaven and I stood with God and I was forever changed. The story of those glorious nine minutes, and of the difficult, sinful, mixed-up life that led to them, is a story I told in my first book, *Waking Up in Heaven*. And since that book came out I've read thousands and thousands of letters from people who tell me all the ways they relate so deeply to my story. Not just the heaven stuff, but everything that came before it—the fears and the doubts and the bad decisions that defined who I was for my first thirty-three years on earth.

I've heard from teenagers who are lost, like I was, and single mothers who are struggling, like I did.

I've heard from women wrestling with the terrible consequences of abortion, same as I did and still do.

I've heard from women bound and broken by child abuse, same as I was for the longest time.

And I've heard from people who want to believe God is real but need more proof—just as I did before I went to heaven.

And what I want to tell these people—what I need to tell them—is that what happened to me *after* I came back from heaven was every bit as life-changing and miraculous as my trip to heaven was.

And best of all, it is something that can happen *to them*. *To you.*

Because ever since December 10, 2009, my life has been profoundly changed. I have been utterly and fundamentally transformed, straight down to the core of who I am. In every conceivable way—heart, mind, soul, and spirit—I am a brand-new person.

By dying, I learned how to live.

And now I know that while heaven is real and our true home and the place we all want to go to someday, we are meant to have meaningful lives full of passion and purpose in Christ right here, right now, this very moment.

We are meant to chase heaven while we're still here on earth.

So how, exactly, do we do that? What does chasing heaven mean?

For me, it meant going to a dark and dangerous strip club. Actually, not just one strip club. *Sixteen* strip clubs.

In one night.

Why?

The short answer is that, after I returned from heaven, I felt a great longing to go *back*—to find a way to be close to God again. I could never just return to the life I had, as beautiful as it was and as much as I loved it. I was different, and my life had to become different, too. Somehow, I had to find heaven again.

And so I started chasing heaven here on earth.

At first, though, I didn't really know what that meant. I didn't know *how* to change my life. I didn't know *how* to chase heaven. And so I did what we all do in moments of need—I prayed. I asked God to bring me closer to Him and to heaven.

"Use me, Lord," I prayed. "Fill me with Your spirit. Mold my heart for Your will. Father, break my heart for what breaks Yours."

And that's just what God did.

The story of *Chasing Heaven* is the story of how God called to me, what He told me, and how I found a way to get closer to Him again.

Even if it meant looking for heaven in places that seemed more like hell.

The experience of dying and going to heaven taught me so many incredible lessons about earthly joy and faith and love. It taught me that the secret to achieving true grace on earth—to finding true peace and happiness—is rejecting a passive, lukewarm love for God and replacing it with a powerful, practical, and purposeful faith in His Word and His way. It is turning our faith from a few smoldering embers into a raging fire.

It is allowing our faith to be *ignited*.

Because the truth is *all of us* can have our faith ignited through God. This is a book for anyone who wants to feel the incredible strength and power of God's love in a very practical, purposeful way in their lives right now.

The message of this book is also that we don't have to die and go to heaven in order to change our lives and ignite our faith. We don't have to abandon the lives we have or empty our bank accounts or move to another country in order to get closer to God and to heaven. It is about each one of us finding a way, given our own lives and circumstances, to go where God calls us to go.

Now, it wasn't easy for me to step out of my safe suburban life and into some dark and desperate corners of the world. Some people might even say it was dumb or naive.

But after I got back from heaven I heard and heeded a call to go into the darkest places there are, so that God could use me to help spread the light of His love there. "And if you spend yourselves in behalf of the hungry and satisfy the needs of the oppressed," God says in Isaiah 58:10, "then your light will rise in the darkness, and your night will become like the noonday."

And when I went into these dark places, I wasn't alone. There was an *army* of others out there who were already spreading the light of God's love in the places where it is needed most.

It wasn't always a huge army—sometimes it was just a handful of other moms and wives and women just like me.

But it was an army nonetheless, because these people were fierce and fearless warriors for God. These people didn't all die and go to heaven and come back, like me—in fact, none of them did. And they don't all spread the light of God's love in the same way—some literally go into dark places; others comfort people who live within their own darkness.

But what they all have in common is a firestorm of faith.

They are all leading purposeful, ignited lives.

They are all finding a way to get closer to God here on earth.

And it is through them I discovered what it means to truly chase heaven.

CHAPTER ONE

Code Blue

NOT TOO LONG AGO, MY SIX-YEAR-OLD DAUGH-
ter Willow lost a tooth. She was a little shaken up until I told
her the good news—she was eligible for her very first visit from the
tooth fairy. That evening, when I put Willow to bed, she couldn't
have been more excited. But because she is her mother's daughter,
she was also a bit anxious.

"Mom, did you write the note to the tooth fairy?" she asked
me more than once.

"You bet I did, sweetie."

"Mom, how little is she?"

"Very little."

"Oh my goodness, Mom, do you think she'll be able to fit
under my pillow?"

"For sure she will."

"Did you call her to tell her about my tooth or does she just
know?"

"She just knows, munchkin."

"Mommy," Willow finally said, after giving the matter much thought, "it's such a pretty tooth and I love it because it's *my* tooth, so can you put on the note to just leave me the money and not take my tooth?"

It's gonna be a long night, I thought.

My husband, Virgil, and I finally managed to get Willow to sleep, and we both enjoyed how excited she was. I even liked that she tried to find a loophole in the child/tooth fairy contract. One of the great joys of having children is that they allow you to relive the magical moments of your own youth, and Willow's enthusiasm about the tooth fairy—her pure and perfect innocence— warmed my heart. Some of my fondest childhood memories are of lying in bed on Christmas Eve hoping to hear Santa's sleigh or waking up Easter morning ready to find the eggs the Easter bunny left behind. When I was Willow's age, I had no problem believing in the tooth fairy or the Easter bunny or Santa Claus or any other mythological figure.

The one being I couldn't fully believe in, though, was God.

In order to understand the absolute glory of what happened to me in heaven and beyond, you need to understand how lost and broken I was in my life before I died.

I was a sinner and a skeptic and I believe I broke every one of God's Ten Commandments. Not just most of them—every single one. Think about that for a moment. Think about how many bad decisions it takes to break ten out of ten.

But that's what I did, and that's who I was—busted, damaged, lost. That pure and perfect innocence I saw in my daughter Willow? That was gone by the time I was three. And the reason I had such a hard time believing in God was because I saw so little evidence of Him in my life. The tooth fairy? No problem—lose a tooth, find a dollar under your pillow. *That* was evidence. The Easter bunny brought chocolates, and Santa Claus brought toys—again, evidence. But God? I simply saw no proof that He was real.

Because if He was real, wouldn't He have protected me from all the bad stuff?

Where was the evidence of God in my life?

I grew up in a small, flat town near an air force base in southwestern Oklahoma, not far from the Wichita Mountains. My mother, Connie, was strawberry blond, beautiful, and full of life, while my father was handsome and charming and always called me "Sugar Bear." As a kid I was a talker, a questioner—I was curious to know why the world was the way it was. I talked so much and asked so many questions, my first-grade teacher couldn't figure out what to do with me. Finally she devised a plan—she cut a piece of loose-leaf paper into five strips and handed them to me.

"Crystal, every time you want to say something, you have to give me one of the strips of paper," she told me. "When the last strip is gone, you can't talk anymore for the rest of the day."

I think it took me less than fifteen minutes to turn over the first four strips of paper. When I was down to my last one, I came up with my own plan. I cut the final strip into five smaller strips, which meant I could talk five more times! Or so I thought, until the teacher took away all my strips and told me to be quiet for the rest of the day.

I got into lots of trouble by always asking the question, "What would happen if . . . ?" For instance, when I was three years old and in day care, I wondered what would happen if I stuck my metal hair clip in an electrical socket. The answer—you get jolted backward ten feet and your fingertips turn black.

Another time, at ballet class, I wondered what would happen if I hurled myself across the slick dance floor at a group of girls in tutus on the other side of the room. The answer—you knock over a bunch of tiny ballerinas, and your mom gets asked not to bring you back to ballet class.

Then there was the time I kidnapped a girl. She was in my day care group, and when no one was watching, I smuggled her onto the bus that took me to my kindergarten class. Then I brought her to my classroom for show-and-tell. Not so she could *see* the show-and-tell, but so she could *be* my show-and-tell. That did not go over so well with the principal.

The big dividing line in my young life, however, happened when I was two years old, and my parents divorced. They married way too young (she was twenty-two; he was twenty), and in the end they just weren't able to fix what was broken. My mom remarried a short time later, to a diesel mechanic who became my stepfather, Hank. He wasn't a terrible guy, and I very much remember loving him, but after his brother was found murdered and he felt let down by the legal system, he turned to drugs and alcohol to quiet his demons. My mom tried her best to love him through it, but things came to a head one night when Hank took his gun and fired it into the bedroom where I was sleeping.

"There," he told my mom, who came running at the sound of the blast, "I killed her."

Actually, he missed me, most likely intentionally, as a way to terrify my mother. It was a turning point in our lives. My mom scooped up my baby brother, Jayson, and me and fought her way out of the house, never looking back.

Sadly, my life only got harder from there. When I was three years old, I was sexually abused. When it happened again, and by more than one person, I just assumed I was to blame. Something had to be wrong with *me*. The shame and guilt I felt became chains that bound me and kept me silent for years and years, well into adulthood—all the way up to the day I died.

And that entire time, I felt completely dirty and broken—beyond all hope and repair.

Chaos was my normal. My mother took me to church and Sunday school every single week, and I heard a lot about God and how loving and compassionate He was, but none of the sermons seemed to apply to my life in the slightest. The concept of a devoted father figure was foreign to me. My own father was absent from my life due to the divorce, and my stepfather had his own issues, so I simply couldn't comprehend the notion of a loving, watchful father. As my feelings of shame and worthlessness took root in my soul, so did my doubts about God.

Now Jesus, He was another story. I remember being eight years old and racing to the front of our old Baptist church as the pastor led the alter call. He said that Jesus would save me and cleanse me, and those were two things I desperately, desperately needed. That night, I was baptized at church, but when the sexual abuse continued, I didn't feel cleansed anymore. So I was baptized again and again and again—four times before I even turned twelve! But nothing ever changed; nothing ever washed away the stains of shame and worthlessness in my heart.

As I got older I grew angry and defiant, and I fought with my mother all the time. I would rage at the world around me because I could not escape the turmoil that was inside me. Over time the fights with my mom got worse, and so I ran. I moved three states away to live with my father in Illinois. My relationship with my dad was complicated: I didn't see him much, and even when I did we had a hard time bonding. He ran a nightclub, so even when I lived with him in Illinois he worked long hours and was gone most of the time. Looking back, I know he tried his best, and I know he loved me, and today we are closer than ever. But when I ran away to live with him, all I was hoping for was a chance to start over.

But the funny thing about running away is that it doesn't matter how fast you do it or how far you go, in the end, there *you* are. It was then, at the age of just thirteen, that I tried to take my life by swallowing handfuls of unmarked pills. The attempt was unsuccessful, and my trudge through the darkness continued.

That was just one of many more bad choices I would make.

After a while I moved back in with my mother. But my continued defiance landed me in the back of a police car, twice, and finally in a home for troubled kids for a night. I turned to drugs and alcohol to numb the pain, and I turned to men for the same reason. At seventeen, I became pregnant. Looking back, I would come to realize that people who feel as if they have no worth behave as if they are worthless.

As rough as things were, there were many moments of great beauty in my life, too. When I told my mother I was pregnant and braced for her reaction, she surprised me by gently putting her arm around me, pulling me close, and crying with me.

"This does not define you," she whispered to me. "You keep your head held high, always."

My mother became a rock of support for me during the pregnancy, and even more so after my beautiful baby boy Jameson Payne was born. But the sad truth was that I often repeated the same bad choices I'd already made. At nineteen, I found out I was pregnant again. Panic raced through me and fear took over. Unable to face my parents or the truth of my situation, I made the heartbreaking, horrifying, life-altering decision to have an abortion. That day, in that clinic, my spirit was finally broken into a million pieces. When it came to God, I had long since felt I had only two options—either He was real and didn't love me, or He wasn't real at all.

Walking out of the clinic, I remember thinking, *If God is real, how could He ever love me now?*

Afterward, I felt like an absolute failure of a human being. I was convinced that I could never, ever be forgiven for this sin. I began to hate myself so much that whenever I passed a mirror I had to look away. I simply couldn't bear to see my own reflection.

From then on, the only God I could possibly believe in was a God Who would wreak vengeance on me for all my horrible sins. A *punishing* God. When bad things happened, I began to see them as God's doing—and many bad things *did* happen.

In my early twenties I got married and had another child, my beautiful daughter Sabyre, but my husband lapsed into drug addiction and the marriage soon fell apart, leaving me broke and alone with two young children. One terrible day in

2002, a former boyfriend came by my house to pick up some of his things and, without my permission, took my son Payne, then six, for a ride on his motorcycle. A few minutes later, I heard sirens. I ran out of the house and yelled my son's name, and before long I arrived at a street blocked off by a police car parked sideways.

That's when I saw my son's tiny black sneakers—the ones with the Velcro straps because he didn't know how to tie his laces yet—lying on their sides in the street. To this day, the images of that moment still flash in my mind—the shoes, the blood, the broken glass, the firefighter sitting on the curb with his head in his hands, crying.

The motorcycle had collided with a pizza delivery truck and my little boy had been thrown under the truck. He was thrown at such a speed that his little head wedged inside the front wheel well and he dangled there, his legs and tiny arms limp like a rag doll's. The firemen arrived and one of them crawled beneath the truck and sawed through the fender well to free Payne. *This is my punishment*, I immediately thought. *God is punishing me for what I did.* Miraculously, my son survived, though the crash took away his hearing in his right ear and left him with injuries he still grapples with many years later. For a long time I believed I was to blame for what happened, and that my son was now suffering for my sins.

Then, in my twenties, I had something beautiful and remarkable happen to me. After the accident with Payne, I swore off dating. My entire focus was on my children and providing for them. I worked two jobs and went to college full-time, in between trips to see doctors and therapists for Payne. But my life took a new turn one evening when I drove onto the air force base in town to meet a girlfriend, and a security officer said something to me while I waited for clearance.

"You going on a date or something?" he asked me.

The first thing I noticed was his beautiful smile. He had light brown skin and piercing brown eyes and before the crash he was the kind of guy I would have fallen for immediately.

"That's none of your business," I snapped. "You don't need to know that to give me a pass, do you?"

"I'm sorry, miss," the guard replied, still smiling. "I didn't mean it that way. I just think you look beautiful."

We were married within a year.

Virgil McVea—a proud, beautiful, strong-willed, God-fearing Christian—is one of the great blessings of my life. He showered me with love and attention and became a caring, genuine father to my two kids. Early on I told him everything about my past—in an effort, I think, to convince him he was too good for someone like me. I even told him about the sexual abuse and the abortion, shameful secrets I hadn't shared with anyone.

"You have survived all that," is all Virgil said, "and you have become the person I love."

Virgil was the first Christian man I ever dated, and his faith was a huge surprise to me. I was a skeptic and a doubter, but his belief in God never wavered. We regularly attended church together, and I wanted so badly to believe Virgil when he told me God loved me, but I simply couldn't fathom it.

Even worse, because of my past, I had trouble trusting men, including Virgil. That lack of trust strained our marriage at first. My mouth was vicious and my words often cut him deeply. I opposed him at almost every turn. When he wanted to give money away to our church or to help others, I fought against it or flat-out refused. Virgil was kind and thoughtful and giving, but I was selfish and concerned with only our own well-being. But over time, Virgil's shining example, and his love for me, led me to give him something I'd never given anyone—my complete trust.

My life was good. I had a loving husband, two amazing kids, and a job as a teacher. For the first time in my entire life, I felt like I was standing on solid ground. Five years into our marriage, Virgil and I decided to try for a baby. We were unable to get pregnant on our own, so we sought the help of a fertility clinic. Before our first appointment, I went into the bathroom, locked the door, sat down, and cried. I pleaded with God—a God I wasn't even sure was listening—not to punish Virgil because of my past mistakes. Then I began to bargain with God. I pushed Him to prove to me once and for all that He was real.

"If we get pregnant," I said, "then I'll know You're real."

A few weeks after my doctor visits and endless shots and tests, we took the pregnancy test in the same bathroom where I had prayed and pleaded with God. Sure enough, I was pregnant.

Later that night, after Virgil had fallen asleep, I slipped back into the bathroom to pray again. I still wasn't convinced that my getting pregnant was truly God's work. I needed even more proof.

"I will really know that You are real," I said, "if we are having twins."

Several weeks later, in the doctor's office, I lay on the examining table looking at an ultrasound screen.

"There is your baby," an attendant said, but before I could even smile she added, "and there is baby number two."

My husband, who is the most gorgeous black man you'll ever see, turned as white as me and said to the nurse, "You can stop counting now."

I threw my hands on my face and cried. It was almost more than I could believe. And yet . . . late that night I retreated to my newest prayer room with yet another request.

"I don't know what is going on," I said to God, "but I will really, *really* believe You are real if we have a boy and a girl."

At fifteen weeks, another ultrasound confirmed we were having a son and a daughter.

Believe it or not, that *still* wasn't enough for me and I *still* wasn't through with the requests. It was all just too much of a coincidence for me.

"God," I said, "I will really, *absolutely* know You are real if one baby has blue eyes and the other has green."

Look, I know how ridiculous this all sounds. God is not a salesman we can bargain with. He is not a genie in a bottle waiting to grant our every wish. This is one of the reasons that I truly love God so much now. When I was so very lost and in such desperate pursuit of Him, I set up these absurd hurdles for Him to overcome to prove to me that He was real. And He did. Back then I thought what I was doing was chasing God. But in reality it was God Who was chasing me. The problem was, I just couldn't see it.

Especially when things began to fall apart.

At only twenty-one weeks, I began to have contractions. I left my job as a schoolteacher and was placed on strict bed rest. I spent my days watching my tummy move as my precious babies rolled and kicked. Four weeks later, I felt a crippling burst of pain in my stomach. Virgil rushed me to the doctor, and I was put in an ambulance and sent 150 miles to a hospital that had a neonatal intensive care unit. There, the doctors confirmed I was experiencing a placental abruption, which meant the placental lining was ripping away from the walls of my uterus. It was a very serious condition that could prove fatal for all three of us.

I had an emergency C-section. The last thing I remember was the oxygen mask coming over my face as I said one last prayer for my babies. I woke up in a recovery room, not knowing what had happened to the twins.

"The babies are here," Virgil told me as he held my hand and kissed my forehead. "They're really little, but they're here."

Virgil wasn't kidding. At birth, my son Micah weighed just three pounds. My daughter Willow weighed only two. They were tested and given Apgar scores, which measure health and vitality on a scale of zero to ten, with ten being completely healthy and zero being all but dead.

Willow got a six. Micah got a one.

My babies showed almost no signs of life. They didn't wiggle around or move their tiny hands and feet. They didn't spit or gurgle or open their eyes. They didn't even make the barest of sounds. We weren't allowed to hold them or even touch them for several days. All we could do was sit beside their incubators and watch them and pray. The doctors gave us little to no encouragement about their survival. It was at that point that Virgil and I both stopped praying.

I ended my last prayer by saying, "God, if You take one of my babies I will hate You for the rest of my life."

Virgil ended his final prayer with, "Father, Your will be done."

From then on, the babies grew stronger every day. After nearly two weeks, we were finally allowed to hold them for the first time.

As I held Micah that morning, he opened his little eyes. Later that day I held Willow as she briefly opened hers, too. And it was in those two miraculous moments that I should have found, once and for all, my belief in God, for as I looked at my precious babies I noticed that Micah had the most beautiful blue eyes I'd ever seen, while Willow's eyes were a wonderful shimmering green.

Unfortunately, like I had so many times before, I convinced myself this occurrence was nothing more than a coincidence, and when I did, I let God slip through my fingers yet again.

After three long months, we got to bring our twins home. Everything was falling into place. I had a great husband and a beautiful family, and my heart was bursting with love for them all. And in turn, they loved me and cherished me, and everything was just as it should be, and I was happy, truly happy, for the first time ever in my life.

Except that something still didn't feel right.

Deep down inside, I still felt dirty and broken. I felt unworthy of all the happiness. I was still bound by the chains of shame and despair, by the weight of my awful secrets. None of that had gone away. It was all still there, locked deep in the core of who I was.

I began to push away the people closest to me. I harbored grudges, shouldered burdens, and wasn't quick to forgive. I still viewed the world through negative and cautious eyes. I didn't believe that God loved me or that I was even close to being worthy of love, anyway. I was still lost, still a sinner, still a skeptic.

Finally, God collided heaven and earth to prove to me how very wrong I'd been.

On December 8, 2009, I went to the doctor for a routine medical procedure. There were complications, and I was admitted to the hospital with pancreatitis. I was placed on a pain pump that administered calculated doses of pain medication as well as a saline drip to keep me hydrated. Two days later, I cried out from my bed in agonizing pain. I felt like I was burning up. My mother sat beside me and gently wiped beads of sweat off my forehead. The doctors assured us everything was fine, but I felt impossibly heavy and groggy. Out of the blue, I asked my mother, "What year is it?"

"What year do you think it is?" she replied.

"It's 1984."

"Well, honey," my mom said with a laugh, "I'm in 2009, so you better come on back here."

Then I told my mother I loved her, and I closed my eyes and began to sink into the deepest sleep I'd ever felt.

I don't remember anything that happened next in that hospital room. Everything I know about it, I was told by someone else. The pain pump had not been set properly, and far too much painkiller was being pushed through my body. My mother touched one of my feet and noticed it felt cold. She pulled a blanket over me, and she saw my lips were turning blue. She listened for my breathing but couldn't hear it; she felt for a pulse but couldn't feel it. Then she screamed for the nurses, who called a Code Blue—the most serious code there is.

A Code Blue means someone is dying. That someone was me.

A doctor rushed in and pounded on my chest. A nurse put a mask on my face and began pumping air into my lungs with an Ambu bag. My mother huddled at the foot of my bed and prayed. I was in full respiratory arrest. My brain, my lungs, my body were all shutting down. I was thirty-three years old, and I was slipping away.

But I don't remember any of it. Because the very instant I closed my eyes in that hospital room, I opened them again in heaven.

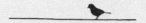

CHAPTER TWO

Heaven

WHEN WE DREAM, OUR DREAMS ARE MURKY AND fuzzy—only a shadow of what real life is like. Real life is substantially more vivid than our dreams. But as vibrant as our experience of real life is, it is only a shadow of what I experienced in heaven. In heaven, everything is infinitely brighter and realer and much more brilliant than it is on earth.

It's as if our life here is the dream, and heaven is the true reality.

When I opened my eyes in heaven, I knew immediately where I was. In fact, in an instant, a complete knowledge of everything was given to me, almost like a download directly into the core of my being. I knew I had left my physical body and was now in a complete and perfect spirit form. But I also knew I was still "me"—the same Crystal who had existed on earth and just died in that hospital room. The "me" that had existed from the first moment God created me. In that moment, standing in the beautiful glow of heaven, I realized I was the most perfect version of myself—the eternal me, free of all the doubts, fears, and insecurities. I felt certain of how I fit into the vast and beautiful universe created by the same God Who breathed life into me.

In heaven, we get to meet our true selves for the first time.

I also felt something that I hadn't felt on earth since the age of three—I felt clean. I was bathed in the most brilliant, beautiful light that could possibly exist—so white and pure and so *cleansing* that it is far beyond any earthly understanding we might have of light and brightness. Being in this light infused me with a sense of purity, cleanliness, and perfection, not to mention love, joy, and happiness. The light was something I could not only see but also *feel*. The light became a part of me, and I became a part of the light. The light was where I belonged—where we *all* belong.

I knew I was home.

When I opened my eyes in heaven, I was also instantly aware that I was not alone.

There were two distinct beings in front of me, standing slightly to the left. They had vaguely humanlike forms—long and slender. The one to the right was a bit taller than the one on the left. I couldn't make out any features, just a brilliant silhouette glowing with a beautiful golden light.

Instantly, I knew who they were—they were my angels.

And instantly, I was overwhelmed by love for them.

I knew that these two beings in front of me were my protectors, my teachers, my heroes, my best friends, my everything. They had been with me always and they would be with me forevermore. They were an inseparable part of my journey through existence, and now they were here to greet me as I arrived in heaven. And once again I didn't just see them—I *felt* them. I was infused by their love and compassion. A complete and instant communication passed between us. The fact that I ever felt lonely on earth seemed unfathomable, given what I now realized in heaven—that I had never, ever actually been alone, that my angels had been there with me for every step along the way and every tear of heartbreak and sadness. Our relationship was pure and perfect—no lies, no shame, no misunderstandings, no apologies. Just love—wonderful, healing, nourishing, beautiful love.

Heaven taught me that we all have guardian angels, and that they never, ever leave our side.

No sooner was I aware of my angels than I became attuned to another great brightness. This brightness had no distinct form, no face or body, not even a shape—the best way I can describe it is to call it a blinding profusion of love. And just as the brilliant light of heaven made me realize instantly that I was home, this blinding abundance of love made me realize what was happening.

I was in the presence of God.

And in this moment I knew that I wasn't *meeting* God. I *recognized* God. My spirit already knew its Creator, the Father for Whom I had longed my whole life. I was filled with the deeply profound certainty that everything around me—the light, the brightness, the angels, the communication—was a creation of

God. I understood that God *is* everything. And I realized, with unsurpassable joy, that I was God's creation, too. I felt the indescribable miracle of being intertwined with Him. I felt closer to God than I ever thought possible, and yet I felt the need to get even *closer*. I was completely humbled by His presence, and I felt an absolute and total surrender to His greatness.

Without hesitation, I collapsed in worship of Him. Not like I worshipped Him in church, by singing or mouthing the words to a prayer—no, I *truly* worshipped Him. I wished to devote every last fiber of my being to worshipping Him. And though on earth I had so many questions I wanted to ask God—"Where were You when I was abused?" "Why didn't You protect me?" "Why do You let so many bad things happen to Your children?"—in heaven, outstretched before Him and in complete and utter awe of Him, I had only one simple question for God.

Why didn't I do more for You?

In heaven, all my questions were answered without my even asking them. God's plan was revealed to me to be perfect in every conceivable way. On earth I didn't understand why bad things happen, but in heaven everything was absolutely clear. All that remained for me to do was to question why *I* hadn't done more. My feelings of inadequacy and failure to live up to God's glory were not negative feelings—in heaven, nothing is negative. They were just part of the complete surrender of myself to God. I didn't feel regret, and I understood my question didn't even have an answer. It wasn't even really a question at all. It was simply a way for me to convey that God deserved so much more from me, because His love for me was so complete.

Along with my realization that I was with God and my angels, I became aware of the majestic beauty of the tunnel of light we were standing in. Many descriptions of heaven include passage through a tunnel. I had imagined the tunnel as a dark, blackened place. Nothing could have been further from what I experienced. For me, the tunnel was a swirling, shimmering circle of brightness, too brilliant for human words to describe. At the end of the tunnel was an even greater radiance, a sparkling, pearlescent coloring that seemed to drawn me to it. I understood immediately what the burst of radiant light was—it was the entrance to heaven.

Then, as I lay outstretched before Him in worship, a peaceful, effortless communication passed between God and me. I was aware that once I made it to the end of the tunnel, I would be irreversibly home.

"Once we get there," God said, "you cannot come back."

Here, two separate emotions flooded through me. The first was sheer joy and elation. I wanted to go through the gates of heaven more than I'd ever wanted anything before. But the other emotion had to do with my four children. It was then that another communication passed between us, and God showed me a vision of my children, and He filled me with the assurance that they would be okay without me should I choose to continue on my journey toward heaven. God poured into my spirit the certainty that His plan for my children's lives, though not without heartaches or trials, was perfect. That I was not truly leaving them, just as He never leaves us. I knew I would still get to watch them grow and love and live, and that, in a way, I would be even more a part of their lives than I was before.

And God spoke to the core of my heart by assuring me that I

would be rejoined with my children again, for eternity, with Him.

God was giving me a choice—stay and be my children's mother or continue toward the gates with Him. And once again, without words, a perfect understanding passed between us.

"God, I want to stay with You."

How could I not want to return to my children? How could I not want to be with my family? All I can say is that being with God was where I belonged. That is not to say I do not love my children with my entire heart. I simply loved God more. The decision I made was the only decision I *could* make. I wanted nothing more than to continue toward the gates, into my eternity.

In the tunnel, God, my angels, and I continued toward the beautiful gates. My attention, though, was diverted by what I saw ahead of me. There was something else God wanted to show me.

It was another being, another presence. It was different from my angels—it had a much more distinctly human form. In fact, unlike every other entity I had encountered in heaven, this figure was fully human.

It was a little girl.

She was small and no more than three or four years old, and she was wearing a white bonnet and a frilly white summer dress with sparkling yellow flowers. She was carrying a white wicker basket. She was skipping and dancing and laughing, just like little kids do on earth. She began dipping her basket into the brightness of the light at her feet, as if it were a resplendent pool of water. She filled her basket with the brightness and poured it out, and the brightness cascaded like a waterfall at her feet. And every time she dipped the basket, she threw her head back and laughed a little girl's wonderfully innocent laugh.

And as I watched her, I felt myself begin to absolutely swell with love for this little girl.

I cannot ever hope to describe how much I loved this child. I have never felt an earthly love as intense as the love I had for her. The love I felt just kept swelling and building and growing and intensifying, until I believed I would explode. This sensation of nearly bursting is one of the most vivid sensations I retain from my time in heaven. I wanted to watch the little girl play and laugh and dip her basket for the rest of eternity, so deep was my love for her. I had never seen anything so pure, so perfect, so beautiful.

And in that instant, as I prepared to shatter into a million pieces, God took away the immense feeling, allowing me to see the little girl more clearly and to understand who she was.

The little girl with the golden basket of light was me.

I understood immediately that what God was showing me in heaven was what He'd been trying to show me all my life on earth.

God was allowing me to see myself through His own eyes, *as He sees me.*

God was showing me that in His eyes I am His pure and perfect little girl, that I was never less than that and never would be. All the self-doubt and self-loathing and insecurities I'd felt on earth were, in that moment in heaven, obliterated. I had no choice but to see and accept the absolute perfection of my creation at God's hands, as embodied by the little girl in that tunnel. She was perfect, the apple of His eye, worthy of His love not because of anything she had done but because she existed. In that moment, God freed me from a lifetime of lies with one simple truth—I was His all along, and all along He had loved me. No matter how much I believed myself undeserving of God's love, He showed me that I *did* deserve it, because *all* God's children are deserving of it. The chains of shame and worthlessness that had bound me most of my life suddenly broke away, undone by the glory and redemption of Christ, as I stood in heaven.

Of course, God showed me myself at three years old for a reason—I was three when the sexual abuse began. God took me back to the very moment when my earthly innocence was lost, in order to show me that my heavenly perfection had never been lost at all. Finally, *finally*, I was cleansed and completely made new in His truth.

In heaven, God took the shattered pieces of who I'd become and made me whole again.

Then I heard a voice I instantly recognized.

"Crystal!" I heard. "*Crystal!*"

It was my mother calling to me from the hospital room back on earth. The sound was so sharp and so abrupt that I knew she was screaming.

For the first time in heaven, I had the sensation of stopping— of something halted. My mother didn't know where I was, or that I was safe. No one on earth did. And this insight began to crowd out the rest of the perfect and beautiful awareness I had been filled with in heaven. I understood that I needed to go back and tell my mother where I was and that I was okay. And as I communicated this to God, I understood His response, which was, "The choice is up to you."

I had to choose. I could either continue down the beautiful tunnel and into my eternity, or I could turn back toward my earthly life. For the first time I looked below me, and I saw the very floor of heaven, like an endless blanket of shimmering water crystals, brilliant like a billion perfect diamonds, a sea of glowing, transparent glass. I became aware of what lay beneath the floor—my earthly home. I knew that beneath me a team of doctors was frantically working to restart my body, and I knew my mother was crying in a corner of the room, begging me not to leave her. Her love for me and her prayers for my return made my spirit long to comfort her. I made my choice, and I slowly turned away from the gates of heaven. And as I focused on the floor, another communication passed between God and me, the most powerful one yet.

"Tell them what you can remember."

"I'm going to remember everything," I called back to Him over my shoulder. "I will be right back."

And then I opened my eyes again, and I was back in my hospital room.

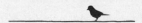

The first thing I saw was a human face hovering above my own, only a few inches away. It was one of the nurses.

"Do you know where you are?" I heard her ask. "Do you know what day it is?"

Yes, I thought, *of course I do. I know everything.* I remembered every detail of where I had just been. I wanted to answer her, but

I couldn't. The words wouldn't come out. It was like I'd forgotten how to speak. Then I saw another face—my mother's face.

"I am in the most beautiful light," I mumbled to my mom. "I am with God."

"I know, I know," my mother said. "But I need you to get back here with me."

And then I closed my eyes, fully expecting to return to heaven. I could feel my spirit fighting to escape my body, and I could feel it being pulled back as the doctors continued to revive me. I distinctly felt myself being pulled farther and farther away from heaven by the people in that room. I closed my eyes again and tried my hardest to go back, but I couldn't. A doctor in a white coat came over and stood above me, holding a syringe.

"Crystal, I'm going to give you some medication that is going to counter the effects that you are experiencing," he said. "On a pain scale of one to ten, this is going to be a ten."

The doctor stuck me with the needle and I felt an immediate surge of horrible pain. Every muscle in my body clenched tight. The pain radiated through my body, building in intensity, surging into my every pore, ripping through me, and tearing me apart like a giant freight train.

"It's almost over," I heard the doctor say.

I gritted my teeth against the pain, both the immense swell of physical pain and the unbearable reality that with every second in that hospital room I was slipping farther and farther away from heaven.

Then it was over. The decision had been made.

And heaven slipped away.

CHAPTER THREE

Be Bold, Be Brave

I HAVEN'T ALWAYS BEEN THE BRAVEST PERSON ON the block. There are maybe a small handful of times in my life that I can look back on and say, "Okay, that was kind of brave." Like the time I was the first person to come across a mangled car wreck on the highway. It was a terrifying sight, but I pulled over and managed to dial 911 with shaking hands. Unfortunately for my ten-year-old daughter, who was in the car with me, I was also screaming as I threw myself in front of the first passing car to get them to stop and help. I later found my sweet daughter curled up into a ball on the floorboard. The crash hadn't scared her—I had. It's honestly a miracle that kid grew up and didn't need therapy.

I admire the kind of people who find themselves in those kinds of difficult situations and just jump into action, cool as ever. My husband, Virgil, is that kind of person. Maybe it's the military training in him that turns him into a G.I. Joe kind of hero during a crisis, while I turn into something that resembles a fainting goat. Virgil is the one you want to call for help in an emergency, not me.

I remember crying so hard on the first day of school because of the overwhelming fears that surged through my body. Fear that the kids wouldn't like me. Fear that I didn't look okay. Fear that my words wouldn't come out right. Walking into that classroom was the last thing in the world I wanted to do.

But I had to, because I was the teacher.

I may not be the bravest person around, but God did give me a very sarcastic sense of humor that seems to get me through tough situations when my courage is lacking. Anytime I'm in a position that provokes large amounts of emotion, I tend to do one of two things—laugh hysterically (even if nothing is funny) or say something wildly inappropriate, neither of which goes over very well at funerals or in a court of law. What can I say? It's a character flaw. On the plus side, my family gets great enjoyment out of watching me try to navigate through these sticky situations.

Like the time I nearly threw up on national television.

I'd been asked the same questions many, many times since I died and went to heaven, and on a spring day in April 2013 I was asked it again.

"What does God look like?"

The difference this time was that I was in front of millions of people.

I was a guest that morning on the show *Fox & Friends*. I was there to talk about my first book and my time in heaven. Needless to say, I had never been on live television before. I live in a small town in western Oklahoma and I'm a schoolteacher. My life and career path had not prepared me for such a moment at all. Yet there I was, sitting on a big yellow couch across from Fox host Gretchen Carlson, with a camera beaming me into homes across the country.

The very last thing God said to me while I was in heaven was, "Tell them what you can remember." Over time I had realized God didn't want me to just tell my heaven story—He wanted me to tell my *whole* story, sins and all. That's what I did in my first book, and that's what I hoped to do on national TV, when Gretchen Carlson smiled at me and asked, "What does God look like?"

It wasn't an easy question to answer. One of the hardest things I've had to do is try and explain with words what I experienced in heaven. It has been enormously frustrating, because there is no language or description that truly correlates to what I saw and learned in heaven. For instance, I always use the color white when I describe the light I saw in heaven, but actually what I saw was so much whiter and brighter and more pure and vibrant than any white we experience on this planet. Our language simply isn't expressive enough. Our most powerful words—*perfect, pure, immaculate, resplendent*—don't even scratch the surface. Imagine how hard it would be for you to explain what an orange is to someone who has never seen one—without using the words *orange, round,* or *fruit.* That's how I often feel.

And yet I had no choice but to try and describe what I saw and felt in heaven. After all, that was what God had instructed me to do. My goal was to convey even a tiny fraction of the sheer joy and utter wonder of what it was like to be in God's presence. So I answered Gretchen's question as best as I could.

I told her that seeing God was like standing in the presence of

"an immense brightness I could hear, feel, taste, smell, and touch."
I remember crying when I talked about how God "freed me from
the shame I had felt my entire life." And I remember giggling at
one point, because that's what I do when I feel nervous or emotional—laugh inappropriately. "I don't like public speaking," I
explained to Gretchen, "so it always makes me laugh that this is
what God sent me back to do."

After the segment was over, I came offstage and hugged my
good friend Jennifer, who had traveled with me from Oklahoma
to New York City and was waiting in the wings. I was still shaking with nerves, but Jennifer told me the segment had gone great.
I stopped for a quick hug and photograph with the country singer
Clay Walker, who was also a guest on the show (can you blame
me?) and I apologized to the great Red Sox pitcher Jon Lester,
whom I didn't recognize because I don't watch sports. He smiled
and said, "It's okay with me not being recognized when I'm in
New York City." Evidently being in the Yankees' hometown isn't
always comfortable for him.

All in all, I felt pretty good.

But then, just as Jennifer and I made it back to our hotel, my
cell phone started chiming with email alerts. People were beginning to react to my segment.

Before I walked out on the Fox stage that morning, I'd been
worried about two things—my hair and my weight.

The makeup artist on the show had teased my hair into a little
flip that fell over one side of my face, and she'd sprayed me with a
lot of hairspray, which I never use, and I felt self-conscious about
it. It didn't feel natural or right. I kept telling my friend Jennifer,
who happens to be a hairdresser, "My hair, my hair!" and she kept
reassuring me, "Crystal, it's fine, don't worry."

On top of that, I had my usual concerns about my body.

For much of my adult life I have struggled with my weight. After marrying Virgil in my late twenties, I began to see a therapist to deal with my issues from childhood—specifically, the aftermath of sexual abuse. I gained eighty pounds in the first year of my marriage. I could write a whole other book about my struggles with my weight, but for now let me just state the truth: I was fat. I knew it, and I honestly never thought people would feel the need to point it out to me because, come on, when you're fat, you know you're fat, right?

I also knew that God didn't say to me, "Okay, Crystal, I'm not going to use you until you lose those eighty pounds."

Nope, God was ready right then and there, and like it or not, I had to be, too.

So I picked out the most flattering outfit I could find and I put on some nice lip gloss and I winked at myself in the mirror and said, "Just do what God asked you to do, girlfriend, and you will be okay." What I looked like wasn't important. What mattered was my story.

But then, back at the hotel in New York City, I opened my laptop and looked at my emails.

The first one was from a woman named Peggy who lived in South Texas. Peggy explained that as she was making her bed that morning, she saw a teaser for the next guest coming up on *Fox & Friends*. She said she didn't think much of it until God instructed her to stop everything she was doing and begin to pray for this guest. Peggy told me she spent the entire segment praying for the guest—for me. I found great comfort in the sweetness of her words, and I felt so loved and at peace.

But hers were not the only words waiting for me online. I also read a series of comments beneath a YouTube video of my TV appearance.

"I know she is lying about going to heaven," one person wrote. "She's too fat to fit through the pearly gates."

Wow, I thought. That's harsh. I felt a pang of humiliation. But I giggled as I read it out loud to Jennifer and I said, "Well, I'll have you know, sir, that our spirits are not fat and I'm not worried about getting through the gate." Then I kept reading.

"I can smell her hot dog breath through the TV screen," another person wrote.

I giggled again, this time a bit less, and I said, "Well, can ya, now? I don't even *like* hot dogs." At the same time, I could feel tears trying to fight their way out of my eyes. Still, I kept reading.

"God just spoke to me, and he told me to tell you to put your fork down," read another comment.

Now I wasn't laughing anymore.

"Close the computer," Jennifer said, but before I did, I saw another comment. It was from a man who claimed to be a Christian but who went on to say that "God wouldn't use someone as gluttonous as you." I was stunned, hurt, and humiliated. The comments kept coming, one more vile and hurtful than the next. I felt deep shame and dread wash over me. The worst comment, the one that hurt the most, mentioned my family.

"If I was her kid," one person wrote, "I'd kill myself."

"Seriously, turn off the computer," Jennifer said again, and this time I took her advice. I stood up and without saying a word walked to the bathroom and locked the door behind me. I sat on the cold floor and put my head on my knees and cried. I cried for fifteen minutes. I felt bullied, belittled, and stupid. I felt angry and betrayed. I was cruelly reminded that going public with my story didn't just affect me—it affected my whole family. My husband, Virgil; my teenagers, Sabyre and Payne; and my four-year-old twins, Micah and Willow—more precious to me than I can describe—they were all in this with me, open to ridicule. I'd put everything on the line to write my book and tell my story, including my relationships and my career.

And for what? I thought in that bathroom. *For this? So I can be publicly humiliated? So my family can be, too? God, why did you make me do this?*

I sat on that cold floor and cried for fifteen minutes before I felt the sensation of God's love on me—a feeling of peace and comfort wrapping around me—and I heard God say, "Let's pray for them. Those who are hurt often hurt others. Let's pray for them."

Amid my tears I allowed God to walk me through praying for these people who hurt me so badly. And as I prayed that their hearts be softened, that the hurt inside their hearts be healed, I saw a vision of my Savior stepping in front of me, and I heard Him say, "It is not you they are rejecting; it is Me."

And just like that, all the anger and shame I felt went away.

And in that moment, the Lord became my shield.

I don't really know how to fully explain what happened to me as I sat on the cold tile in the hotel bathroom except to say that critical words from others have never hurt me since.

By then Virgil, back home in Oklahoma, had read the same comments and he called me to see how I was doing. I told him about my moment in the bathroom and I said, "God has already walked me through it."

"You were great on the show," Virgil said. "You are beautiful."

"You're the reason I look like this," I said, and laughed, "because no matter what, you just keep telling me how beautiful I am."

"Because you are," Virgil said.

After that I was fine. Even the next day, when a headline on a news website mockingly referred to me as the author who "Says She Smelled God"—because I'd said on TV that I could hear, feel, taste, touch, and smell Him—I didn't let it get to me. No headline, no Internet comment, had any bearing on what I was sent back from heaven to do. God knew exactly the kind of reaction my story would get, and although I wasn't prepared for it at all, He was. That's why He surrounded me with prayer from my family, friends, and people like Peggy from Texas.

No, I didn't feel very brave in that hotel bathroom. But that didn't matter. God is always really good about reminding me that it's not *about* me. Even my trip to New York City and my appearance on *Fox & Friends* weren't about me.

I was sent to New York City for another reason—a reason the millions of people who saw me on the show couldn't possibly know about, and a reason I didn't even understand myself until I literally ran into it face-to-face.

God's plan for me that day wasn't about what happened on-stage.

It was about what happened *backstage*.

CHAPTER FOUR

Do It Fat, Do It Scared

BACKSTAGE, ABOUT AN HOUR BEFORE MY *FOX &
Friends* segment, Jennifer and I sat in the greenroom of the
Fox studios in midtown Manhattan. The greenroom is where
guests wait until the producers are ready for them. We'd been there
for a while when a fairly well-known actress came in with her assistant. Jennifer and I looked at each other and smiled. The actress
asked her assistant for some water, and the assistant hurried away
to get it. I looked over at Jennifer and giggled.

"I need you to get me some water, too," I joked.

"Yeah, no chance," Jennifer said without even looking up from
her phone. "You aren't famous."

Eventually, a staffer appeared and led us to the makeup room.
Jennifer had worked on my hair that morning, but now I was
going to get touched up by the show's hair-and-makeup artist.
The room was small and cramped—just two chairs and two
mirrors and barely any space to move. I sat in one chair and the
makeup artist came over. She was in her sixties with blondish

hair and a very thin frame. She seemed tense and distracted, and for a while she didn't say anything at all.

Then, with her back toward me and our eyes meeting in the mirror, she asked, "Are you the lady who wrote the heaven book?"

I said that I was.

"Well," the makeup artist said, "I don't know if I believe you."

I was taken aback. I didn't know how to respond, and she didn't give me the chance, anyway.

"Because what kind of God . . . ?" she continued. "What kind of God . . . ?" She was choking up. She couldn't get the words out.

I didn't need her to. With those few words, I understood. "What kind of God . . . ?" was the *same* question that had haunted me and turned me into such a doubter in the past. My version was "What kind of God lets a little girl be hurt so badly?" I screamed it out to Him on the nights that my terrible memories wouldn't stop flashing in my brain—"What kind of God . . . ?" I cried out to Him when I sat beside my newborn twins in the neonatal intensive care unit as they fought for their precious little lives—"What kind of God . . . ?" The same words that thousands of people have shared with me as they search for answers.

"What kind of God . . . ?"

The makeup artist drew in a deep breath and pushed on.

"I'm a good person," she said, tears streaking her face. "I have cancer and the doctors say there is nothing they can do. I'm a good person. I am a good person. I never did anything wrong. So what kind of God . . . what kind of God . . . ?"

She trailed off and dissolved into herself, broken and furious. She had said everything she had the strength to say.

"I get it," I finally said. "I've asked 'What kind of God . . . ?' for more than thirty years. I understand. But here is what I know."

Then I unspooled the story of my life, right there in the makeup chair, just as God had told me to do. Don't just share the heaven stuff—*share it all*. And so I did. I told her about my life and about my hurts. I told her about my deep, deep feelings of worthlessness and shame, and I said to her, "What kind of God would allow all that? Why didn't God protect me?"

And I told her about my time in heaven.

"What I can say is that there *is* a very real place with a very real God Who loves us with a very real love," I said. "Although at times we cannot understand His plan, He showed me that He uses *all* things for His good."

I was talking quickly now, because there was so much to say.

"The questions that you have here on earth," I went on, "will be explained the instant you meet Him in heaven. But by then they won't matter. Because in that place, all that matters is how much He loves us and how much we love Him."

The profoundness of the moment filled me with emotion, and I began to choke up, too. When I finished talking, we were both silent for what seemed like a long time. Finally, the makeup artist spoke.

"Tell me what it's going to be like," she said in a whisper. "Tell me what it's going to be like to die."

I took her hand in mine.

"When the time comes," I said, "the veil will slowly open. It is like holding your breath for a split second and diving into the water. It is quick and it doesn't hurt at all and it is beautiful, more beautiful than you can imagine, and you are never alone, not even for a moment. He is with you through it all. The Lord doesn't wait for us *in* heaven. He escorts us *to* heaven. The transition is instant. The moment you close your eyes here on earth will be the exact moment that you open them in heaven. There is no fear and there is no pain. You are never alone. He is with you through it all."

The makeup artist squeezed my hand and wiped away her tears.

"I'm scared," she said. "I'm not ready. There is more I want to do here."

"Don't be afraid," I told her. "There is nothing to be afraid of."

Then I asked her if I could pray with her.

She came toward me and wrapped her arms around me, putting her head on my chest. I held her frail body tightly, and together we prayed. We prayed for healing, and we prayed that God might take away her fears. We stayed like that for a while, two strangers in a tiny makeup room in a TV studio in New York City. We stayed like that and we prayed and we cried, together.

And then I said, "No matter which one of us goes first, let's make a promise that we will meet at those beautiful gates with God one day."

Just then a staffer poked her head into the room and said, "Two minutes."

That meant two minutes until I was on live television.

I looked at the makeup artist, and she looked at me, and we laughed and scrambled to get me ready. My mascara was running and she quickly fixed it, which left about thirty seconds to do something with my hair. That's how I ended up telling my story for the second time that morning to Gretchen, with the flippy hair and all.

That's the funny thing about God. When God wants us to do something for Him, He doesn't wait until we feel confident or comfortable to call us. God never promised me that sharing what I experienced with Him would be easy or convenient. He never said He could only use me if I was thin or had perfect hair or if I wasn't afraid. And often, at least with me, He doesn't even explain why He's asking me to do something to begin with. This time, to my many protests, He simply said, "It is not about who you are but Who I am. I am with you always."

In other words, do what you have been called to do when He calls you to do it, even if you have to do it fat and do it scared.

What if I had allowed my fears and apprehensions to stop me from being on that TV show? What if I had insisted to my publisher that I wasn't going to appear on any media—that I was too scared or too self-conscious? What if I had allowed an excuse, or several excuses, to stop me from doing what God asked me to do—go out and tell my story?

I know the answer to those what-ifs.

I would never have met the makeup artist.

With God, nothing is a coincidence. Nothing is by chance. God knew that my path would cross with this woman's at that very moment in that makeup room. And He knew that our lives would be forever changed because of that moment together.

A moment when heaven and earth collided.

If we want to be closer to God here on earth—if we want to chase heaven while we're alive—we may have to do it even if we feel uncomfortable and scared. No matter the consequences. When He calls, we must go.

I won't lie—the meanness of those website comments really hurt. I'd spent a lifetime feeling rejected, and there I was being cast off again, this time by total strangers. I already knew I was the least likely candidate to be on national television talking about God. But what I came to realize is that God uses the least likely candidates! God doesn't always call the equipped, but He does always equip the ones He calls. I was someone who was never really popular—I was always picked last, was prone to peer pressure, and practically lived in the principal's office. I was the one who got kicked out of ballet class, dropped out of high school, was a teenage single mother. I was the one looking for love in all the wrong faces. I felt overweight, abused, broken, full of doubts—why would God use me? Of all people, why me?

Because it doesn't matter what we think of ourselves. It matters what *God* thinks of us.

Through the love of God and the redemption of Jesus, I was changed forever. And though I still have many of the same fears and insecurities I've always had—though I am still a completely imperfect human being—I now have the strength to push through those fears and doubts and keep letting God use me for His glory. The meanness may bruise me, but it can never, ever break me.

This is one of the most important lessons that dying taught me about living.

The lesson that, while we may not feel we are worthy, to God we *are*.

God finds us worthy.

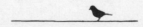

Look at the apostles. The apostles loved the Lord, and they swore they would never abandon Him, and yet, in the garden of Gethsemane that fateful night, one of them betrayed our Savior while the others ran away. Fear got the better of them. Jesus told Peter that he would deny Him, and before the sun rose Peter did just that, three times. Fear got the better of him, too. And when Jesus was crucified outside Jerusalem, only one of the apostles was there for Him. The others were struck by fear.

Fear has that effect on us. It makes us do things we swore we would never do and it makes us not do things we swore we always would. Maybe that's why the Bible tells us so many times not to be afraid—because God knows exactly what blubbering messes we'll become when we are gripped by fear.

And yet . . . when Jesus was resurrected, He built His church upon these same scared, flawed men. He referred to Peter, the apostle who had denied Him, as the very rock of His church. Jesus used someone who had denied Him and run from Him as the foundation of His church! Jesus understood Peter's fear. Jesus knew his heart. But He also knew that Peter, and the rest of the apostles, had been *transformed* by His resurrection, and that they were worthy of carrying His Word and building His church.

Being scared to do something does not make us failures.

It makes us *the exact kind of person* God loves to use.

CHAPTER FIVE

A New Normal

L ONG BEFORE I SAT ON THAT YELLOW COUCH ON national TV, I'd already begun to share my story with the world. In fact, the very first time I told about my heaven experience was literally five seconds after I came back.

"I am in the most beautiful light," I said to my mother in a tiny whisper as she stood over me in my hospital bed.

It was my first testimony.

I also thought it would be my last.

You see, I had every intention of going back to heaven as soon as I told my mother I was okay. That was the only reason I left heaven in the first place. But things didn't work out that way. So many people in my hospital room were talking and yelling and praying and just *willing* me back to life. Their collective efforts pulled me back to earth.

But instead of feeling grateful to them, all I felt was anger.

Why were they doing this to me? Didn't they know all I wanted was to go back and be with God? I fought against them with all my might, but it was no use. I simply couldn't free my spirit from the prison of my body.

Finally I gave up. I opened my eyes and realized I wasn't going anywhere. It felt like a door had been slammed shut. And as soon as I knew I wasn't going back to heaven, my angels, or God, I started to cry.

I was devastated.

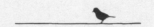

The next few days and weeks were long and difficult. It is not an exaggeration to say that after I died and went to heaven, I had to learn how to live all over again. For quite a while after I woke up in that hospital room, I still felt powerfully infused by God. I still felt the beautiful glow of His presence. There was nothing subtle about it—I missed God terribly and I wanted to be back with Him. I was *pining* for Him.

Very soon after being revived, though, I also began to feel thankful for being back with my sweet family. How could I not? These two powerful feelings—wanting to be with God, but grateful to be with my family—battled each other inside my heart. I felt like I was being torn in half. Anyone who knows me knows that my love for my family is ferocious—I would do anything and everything to protect my children and husband. But even so, God now came first.

Which, in the beginning, didn't exactly thrill my older kids.

I was honest with them. I told them about the choice I made in heaven to stay, and at first it was hard for them to understand. Even today one of them will tease me and say, "Yep, when it came down to it, she didn't choose us. Thanks a lot, Mom." How could

I choose anything over my children? I wouldn't have understood it either, but that was before I found myself in God's presence and everything changed. I instantly understood that the love of God is greater and more powerful than any other kind of love. And I didn't only understand it; I felt it, heard it, saw it, and tasted it with every fiber of my being. When I was in my spirit form, there was simply no other conceivable option for me but to be with God. I was honest with Virgil, too, and early on, I told him I was even mad at him for praying so hard for me to survive.

"Why did you make me come back?" I scolded him. "This was not my choice."

That is how strong the pull and the power of heaven were. They were overwhelming.

The intensity of my feelings for God and for heaven never lessened, but gradually the sense of connection I felt to heaven began to fade. God's presence in my life was as strong as ever, but it is impossible to be in two places at one time, and I had to come to grips with the fact that I wasn't going back to heaven anytime soon. I understood why it had to be that way—because if God had allowed me to keep feeling what I felt in heaven, I don't think I could have survived in this world.

This readjustment was a very deliberate process, and I had to force myself to slip back into the different parts of my old skin. Crystal the mother. Crystal the wife. Crystal the teacher, daughter, friend, and sister. At first, none of it felt comfortable or right. My life felt like it belonged to someone else.

It was around then that I realized my life *did* belong to someone else.

It belonged to the new me.

It took me a while, but I came to understand that being in

heaven had completely transformed me. I was, to put it simply, a brand-new person. Something had fundamentally changed the core of who I was. "Neither do people pour new wine into old wineskins," it says in Matthew 9:17. "If they do, the skins will burst; the wine will run out and the wineskins will be ruined. No, they pour new wine into new wineskins." That was me—I needed a new wineskin. Trying to pour myself back into my old life simply wasn't going to work.

There is a lot of science to back up this kind of personal transformation following a traumatic event. Studies have shown that people who undergo near-death experiences and see or glimpse heaven come back to earth feeling utterly changed and different. Sometimes they are more calm and peaceful. Sometimes they are more loving and compassionate. Sometimes they are different in ways they can't even understand.

That's how it was with me, at least at first. I was different, but I didn't know what that meant or how to handle it.

And so I did what I thought at the time was a reasonable thing to do—I tried to give away every last one of my family's possessions.

It began one night when Virgil found me crying in my bedroom.

"What's wrong?" he asked.

"Virgil, I have to become a pastor!" I said.

My husband laughed, but quickly stopped when he saw that I was dead serious. I told him I felt like a part of me was still in its spirit form and that I couldn't just pretend everything was the way it used to be. I had to share the truth of heaven and God with the world, and I had to share it *right now*, and how else could I do that if I didn't become a pastor?

"You don't need to become a pastor to tell your story," Virgil said calmly. My husband says everything calmly, which is one of the things I adore about him but which also drives me nuts sometimes.

"You don't understand," I went on in a panic. "I have to go to school and become a pastor and go to Africa to become a missionary and spread the Word of God everywhere!"

Never mind that our twins were barely one yet—I was ready to pack up and change continents that night. Virgil laughed again when I said "Africa" because he knew I wasn't the kind of girl who likes to be hot and sweaty or outside of my comfort zone. But that night, I think Virgil realized how much heaven had changed me. And I know that if God had spoken to him and told him we were supposed to go to Africa, he would have packed our bags that night. But the only thing God told my husband was that his wife wasn't crazy, and to love her through some of these hard changes.

Virgil assured me that I would have many opportunities to tell people about the reality of heaven, and slowly the urge to become a pastor and move to Africa went away. But the urge to do something dramatic with my life only got stronger.

One major change after I came back from heaven was that I no longer carried a lot of the emotional baggage I'd been lugging around for years. All my old grudges and grievances went away—I just didn't feel mad at anyone anymore. There was one person in particular who had been a real problem for my family and me in the months before I went to heaven, and now that I was back, I wasn't even angry at them anymore. This person owed us a significant amount of money, and we were caught up in a lawsuit to get our funds back. Out of the blue, I told Virgil I wanted to drop the lawsuit.

"I know we're never getting that money back, and that's okay," I said. "We have to pray for them."

Now, forgiving a large debt—and letting go of old grievances—was simply not like the old Crystal. I was a bit of a pit bull when it came to fighting for what I believed was right. I tended not to let things go—I was keen to settle them. Yet there I was, saying good-bye to the money our family needed and feeling genuine compassion for a person I'd previously wanted to shake by the throat.

Virgil says he never doubted my experience, but he also confesses that this was how he was convinced, beyond all question, that I was telling the truth about heaven.

There were other things I wanted to let go, including all of my stuff. Before heaven, I had been extremely sentimental about objects, and I cherished them as prized possessions. Afterward, that all went away. I felt zero attachment to any material thing. I was so determined to overhaul my life that I proposed to Virgil we give away our home to someone who needed it more than we did.

"Well," Virgil said with a smile, "*we* need our house, too."

Not much later, Virgil came into our bedroom and found me knee deep in a pile of our clothes and shoes I wanted to give away. I saved two outfits for each of us. They were hanging in the closet. That poor, sweet man and what he had to deal with.

"Yeah," Virgil said as he picked up the clothes and hung them back in the closet, "we kind of need these, too."

Still, I was undaunted. If you happened to be my friend at that time, it was the perfect opportunity to come around my house and take anything you liked. My friend Kara would often jokingly say things like, "On a scale of one to ten, just how attached are you to your car?" or "Is God telling you to give me any money?" But I was serious. I was ready to give it all away—every last thing. When I walked to the gates of heaven, I sure wasn't pulling a rolling suitcase behind me. In my time with God we never talked about my new car or how big my house was. The balance in my checking account or how many pairs of shoes I owned didn't matter. When I died I took nothing material from this world with me. What I took was something far more precious, and it didn't have a price tag—I took memories and lessons and adventures and triumphs, and most of all, I took love.

In that moment with God, the only thing that mattered was not what I had but what I had given.

CHAPTER SIX

Free-Falling

I GUESS YOU COULD SAY I WAS CONFUSED. I WAS thrashing around inside of my own mind, trying to fit into my life again. What was my new life supposed to look like? Who was I supposed to be now? God didn't give me a full set of instructions for what to do when I came back from heaven. I was going to have to wing it.

These questions went unanswered for a long time, and I felt like I was pretty much twisting in the wind for the better part of a year after I came back.

And in that time, ever so slowly, without my even noticing it, I was beginning to drift away from my time in heaven. I could still remember it vividly, but it felt further away. The feeling of being half-human, half-spirit disappeared, until one day, despite my resistance, I felt fully human again.

All that remained of my time in heaven were the beautiful memories and the powerful, powerful urge to *do more* for Him.

Eventually, I resumed the home day care I'd managed before I died. I loved being around babies again, and taking care of them made my days pass quickly. And in the evenings Virgil would go off to work his night job (he was a security officer on the military base in our hometown) and I would take care of our tiny twins, Micah and Willow, who weren't yet two years old. Once they fell asleep, I'd slip away to the bathroom, close the door behind me, and start to cry.

"What am I supposed to do?" I'd ask God.

And though I'd heard God's voice in heaven, clear and powerful, back on earth I could no longer hear Him in the same way. That was one of the hardest adjustments of all. At first it made me mad that He wouldn't answer me. "I know You are here!" I'd exclaim. "I know You can hear me!" There were days when I literally begged God to talk to me again.

This struggle went on and on. I kicked and screamed and searched for meaning and came up empty all the time. I cried every single night for the better part of my first year back from heaven. I was mad God had sent me back and not even given me a hint as to why. All I wanted was to feel God as strongly here on earth as I had when I was with Him in heaven. The terrible frustration was in not knowing how to do that.

Every day I felt an overwhelming *urgency* to do something— I just didn't know what.

For starters, I began reading the Bible again. I went into one of our closets and pulled down the thick, hardback Bible that Virgil had used when he was finishing Christian college. It was packed with study guides and history lessons. I lugged it out to the living room, sat down, and put it on my lap. Then I started reading.

I did not start with Genesis 1. I did not start with "In the beginning God created the heavens and the earth." You see, I had tried diving into the Bible before, lots of times, and I'd always started with Genesis and made it through the first book pretty easily. But then inevitably I'd give up before ever starting Exodus. Periodically I'd dip into later parts of the Bible to read something that was required for a class assignment, but I never really read it as I read other books, start to finish.

So this time I started with book two, Exodus.

And this time I kept reading.

It got to where I couldn't wait to get back to reading the Bible. I'd carve out little pockets of free time and pick up where I'd left off. I'd put the kids to bed, kiss them good night, and go right to my book, or I'd wake up, feed the kids, and read at the table while we ate.

But it was also a slow and gradual process. Sometimes I would strongly feel God's presence during my prayer time. But I could also go weeks without hearing or feeling anything at all from Him. Most of the time, all I could do was keep praying and reading, so I did. The books of Exodus, Leviticus, and Numbers. Slowly, all of the books of the Old Testament. And then the New Testament—Matthew, Mark, Luke, and John. First and Second Corinthians and Philippians, on through James, First, Second, and Third John, Jude, and finally to Revelation. It took many months of stealing away to read a page or two, but eventually— and for the first time in my life—I read the full Bible.

This was all part of throwing myself into the kind of Christianity I thought would bring me closer to God. After I returned from heaven, my husband and children and I never missed a single Sunday service. We served on every church committee we could, led Sunday school, hosted Bible studies, and picked up ice cream for the socials. We had our kids go to youth group and church camps, and perform in the annual Christmas play. We were constantly going and doing—our lives became a blizzard of church activities. We became the "yes" people; if someone asked us to do something, we always said yes.

Honestly, trying to be everything we thought God wanted us to be became exhausting after a while.

Let me say right away that a lot of very good things came about because of what we did that year. Churches always need people to serve, and church work is incredibly important. Certainly my kids benefited from all the activities and church camps. Everything we did was wonderful and meaningful, and we learned a lot about ourselves and our faith.

For instance, for the first time, we began praying together as a family. I had been in church my entire life and never, not once, had I ever prayed with my family. Just a few days after returning home from the hospital, I vowed to change that. And so every morning, I began to pray with my kids.

My two oldest children were preteens, and not surprisingly, they weren't too thrilled by our new ritual. I'd grab them as they were rushing out the front door trying to catch the school bus and we'd gather as a family in the living room and hold hands to pray.

"Does anyone feel called to lead prayer today?" I'd always ask.

I'd be met with silence and eye rolls.

So for the first few months back, I was a praying warrior. I ignored the long, exaggerated teenage sighs and pushed on. But as time went on, I felt less like a prayer warrior and more like a prayer failure. My kids didn't seem to be into it at all, and I was sure they thought I was completely lame. Finally, one morning, I didn't meet them in the living room for prayers.

"*Mooommmm,*" my older son, Payne, called through the house. "Come on, we are gonna miss the bus."

"Well, go then," I hollered back.

"But aren't you going to pray for us, Mom?" my daughter Sabyre asked as she rounded the corner into my bedroom, where I was folding laundry.

"Nah, you guys go ahead," I said. "I'm not going to force you to pray with me anymore."

Then something remarkable happened.

Both my teenage children came into my bedroom and took hold of my hands and began to pray. Later on they admitted to me that they'd actually come to like that part of our morning. That evening Sabyre told me that she'd almost missed the school bus. She told a friend it was because we'd been praying together as a family.

"I wish my parents would pray with me," her young friend replied.

That moment in my bedroom with my children, God showed me I wasn't doing such a bad job after all.

Honestly, trying to be the perfect Christian left me feeling a little hollow. Something was still missing. It felt like I was trying to climb up a long ladder so that I could get closer to Him, but the higher I climbed the less I could hear and feel God. I became restless and frustrated. All of a sudden, after a year of climbing, I let go of the ladder and began what I call a free fall into faith.

And it all started with a chocolate bar.

There were times when Virgil would bring home chocolate bars as a treat for the family. It was a thoughtful, beautiful, and caring gesture, but I noticed he always brought home the *one* kind of chocolate bar I didn't like. I know some people will say chocolate is chocolate, and the fact is, I like most every kind of chocolate, but I just didn't like the chocolate he kept bringing home for us.

One night, after about the fifth time he showed up with this particular chocolate bar, I tossed it back at him and said, "Virgil, I really, truly appreciate how you think of me and all that you do for me. But just once I wish you would ask me what I want."

It wasn't my sweetest wifely moment, I'm sure. But I tell this story now because, years later, I realized it parallels how I think God felt about me when I came back from heaven.

I can just see God sitting down next to me and saying, "Crystal, I really appreciate all that you have done this year. But just once I wish you would slow down enough to ask Me what *I* would like you to do."

Once I came to that realization, I let go of the ladder and began my free fall of faith. And like any free fall, it was frightening. I didn't know what God wanted me to do, and yet I had to commit to doing whatever it was He asked of me. I had to surrender my own will and give in entirely to His. I had to step away from all that I knew and all that I'd done and all that I'd been, and free-fall toward something new and unknown. And that, my friends, was scary.

Like walking-on-water kind of scary.

One night, in the midst of my searching, God led me back to read the story of Peter and Jesus on the water.

Peter and the other disciples sat together in a boat as it rocked and swayed on the rough waters. The Bible clearly tells us that the waters were so rough, these professional fishermen who'd spent most of their lives on the water were frightened. They got even more scared when they looked up and saw a figure walking toward them on top of the water.

"Take courage!" the figure called out. "It is I. Don't be afraid."

The apostles knew immediately the voice belonged to the Lord.

Just then, good old Peter piped up.

"Lord, if it is really You, then tell me to come to You across the water," he said.

Jesus obliged Peter and said to him, "Come!"

I can imagine the excitement Peter must have felt as he gently put his feet on the surface of the water and took his first tentative steps away from the boat. But that excitement quickly turned to panic as soon as Peter looked down and noticed the rough waters around him. You see, Jesus had instructed Peter to come, but He had not instructed the waters to calm. And like so many of us do, Peter took his eyes off Jesus and focused instead on the water around him. And when he did that, he began to sink.

"Save me, Lord!" he yelled as he sank.

Jesus reached out His hand and caught Peter to keep him afloat.

"You of little faith," Jesus said to him. "Why did you doubt?"

As I read that part in the Bible, I remember whispering to myself, "Peter failed."

But my Savior spoke tenderly and deeply into my heart and said, "Peter may have started to sink, but at least he got out of the boat when I called. Even when Peter was sinking, he was still closer to Me than those who remained in the boat."

I understood what God was saying. He was asking me if I would step out of the boat—move away from the false sense of safety my life offered me—and into the true safety of His arms. Would I be bold enough to go when He called and keep my eyes fixed on Him? Would I trust Him even if He didn't calm the waters I was being called to walk on?

With a shaky voice, I said aloud, "Yes, Lord, I will."

I began to reflect on how I'd lived my life before heaven. I hadn't been a bad person. I had a good heart and I cared for people. I went to church and sometimes I put money in the collection plate. I bought doughnuts and led the youth group and helped people whenever I could.

But the truth, I realized, lay behind all that. Yes, I went to church, but most of the time, didn't I sit there looking at my watch or writing up grocery lists in my head? I had helped people, but hadn't I helped them only when it was convenient for me? Sometimes I gave money, but wasn't that usually out of fear or guilt and never out of the pure beauty of giving?

I may have appeared to be a good Christian.

But the only thing that was missing was Christ.

The instant I said, "Yes, Lord, I will," God broke through to a place so deep within me, I didn't even know it existed. It was as if nothing I'd ever done mattered until the day I started doing it all for Him. And once my heart was truly open to hearing what He wanted me to do, the answers came quickly. The first thing God did was plant two simple words in my spirit.

Go. Love.

After that, more words came. "Follow Me, Crystal," I heard the Lord say. "Do good in this world. Go and show mercy as I have shown. Feed the hungry, clothe the naked, care for the widowed and orphaned, show compassion on the poor. Fight for righteousness, seek justice, give grace and love as I have loved. Follow Me."

And to all of that, I said yes.

And it was this desire to truly follow God, coupled with my experience of His love and grace, that led me to pray a prayer that would change everything.

"Lord, I do love You and I want You to use me. I want to see others as You see them. I want them to see You within me. Father, guide me and mold me and send me. *Lord, break my heart for what breaks Yours.*"

And that simple prayer wrecked me forever.

That prayer would be the catalyst God used to lead me into some of the dirtiest, darkest, and most beautifully messy places on earth.

It wasn't long after that simple prayer that God began to turn my lukewarm Christianity into a firestorm of faith.

CHAPTER SEVEN

Love Wins

ONE NIGHT NOT LONG AFTER I SAID YES TO THE Lord, I got a phone call from a friend I knew from church. Her name is Briar, and I've liked her from the moment we met. She is always smiling and infectiously positive, and when I'm around her I know I'm going to laugh about something. I connect with Briar on so many levels. She is a single mother who fled an abusive marriage with a newborn baby and a backpack. She got on a Greyhound bus that took her 1,500 miles away from her nightmare and into the unknown. When she stepped off that bus, she stepped into a brand-new life.

I understood some of what she was going through. Many years earlier, I had fled my own nightmare. I was just a baby myself, only twenty years old, when I married my first husband. I was already a single mother, and I was excited by the idea of finally having a family of my own. I had really big dreams for my new family, but sadly none of them came true.

My husband's occasional and secret drug use spiraled into

full-blown addiction. His drug-and-alcohol-fueled rampages took over our lives, though at the time I accepted the insanity of living with an addict as normal. I would learn many things before I finally found the strength to leave. I learned, for instance, what my skin feels like when it's burned by a cigarette. I learned how horrifying it is to have the man who vowed to love and honor you spit in your face. I learned that even a beautiful newborn baby can't always fix what's broken ...

Just weeks after our daughter was born, I tried for the first time to leave my marriage. I say "tried" because despite going to the police and getting help from a women's shelter, I still couldn't completely break away. My husband cried and vowed to change. He swore that he loved me, and I got pulled back in. My hopes were rebuilt, only to be quickly shattered again.

Finally, I bundled my babies up in the dead of a winter night and set out into the cold for help, on foot. My husband had taken or broken everything I owned, including my car, and he had wiped my bank account clean. The only things he left me with were the only things that truly mattered—my children Payne and Sabyre. The three of us set out into the bitter cold for a seven-mile walk to the safety of my mother's house.

I pushed their stroller through the freezing wind and snow. The conditions were much harsher than I'd expected. Walking even one block was brutal. The chill of the air burned my face and I stopped to tuck the blankets up around my babies. I started to cry—hard, pain-filled tears—while my children slept in their stroller and I pushed on through the first mile.

And then, out of nowhere, I saw two headlights in the distance.

The car came toward me and stopped a few feet away. I braced for the worst. The driver-side window rolled down, and I realized the car was a taxi.

"Let me give you a ride, ma'am," the driver said.

I thanked him and told him we were fine.

The driver, an older man with a kind face, got out of the taxi and walked toward us. Once again he offered us a ride.

I told him I had no money.

"Never mind that," he said. "Let's just get these babies out of the cold."

Something about him made me feel safe, and I let him help me get my children into the cab. I told the driver where we were going, and he drove us the rest of the way, more than six miles.

"I can't pay you," I told him again through my tears.

"That's okay," he said. "One day you will do something to help someone else."

And just like that we were saved by an angel disguised as a cabdriver.

I've never, ever forgotten what it felt like to be alone and on the street that freezing winter night, and maybe that's why I have always felt so connected to my friend Briar.

After Briar disembarked the Greyhound bus, she got a job as a secretary at a local college and never looked back. But she got caught in the same trap that ensnares so many single mothers—she made too much money to qualify for assistance, yet not enough to provide everything she needed for herself and her young son. Still, I never once heard Briar complain. She is always thankful to Jesus for everything in her life, and she is kind, faithful, and reliable in all that she does. She became the worship leader at her church, and every Sunday she used her powerful singing voice to usher in the presence of the Lord. I'd often tell her that one day I'd be sitting front row center at one of her concerts.

Briar owned a really beat-up clunker of a car that was falling apart inside and out, and when she called me that night it was because her car had broken down and she needed me to pick her up. It wasn't the first such call I'd received from her.

"Crystal, I hate to ask, but is there any way you could come and get me?" she asked politely through the sound of cars and 18-wheelers ripping past.

And every time her car broke down, she'd find a way to tow it home and have her father work on it. He would patch it up just enough to get it back out on the road. Then she would pray to God to keep it running. It wasn't safe for her to be driving around with her son in such a heap, but she had no other choice.

"Is there any monthly payment you could afford for a new car?" I asked her.

"Yes," she said. "Zero dollars a month."

The only way she would ever be able to replace her clunker, Briar said without a trace of sadness or self-pity, "was if God dropped a new car in my lap."

"Who do you think God is, Oprah?" I joked.

We laughed, even though her situation wasn't funny. Briar truly had no way of replacing her dangerous car. Whatever extra money she could squeeze out of her paychecks went into a fund to buy her son a Christmas present. But because she loved and trusted in God, she was thankful for her clunker, and for her father, who kept it clunking along.

I drove to where Briar was stranded and got her home safely, but afterward I couldn't stop thinking about our conversation. In particular, I thought about what Briar had said about the chances of her getting a new car.

That got me thinking.

What if God *was* to drop a new car in Briar's lap? How, exactly, would He do it? After all, new cars don't just drop out of heaven.

Or do they?

Often, when God asks me to do something, I have absolutely no idea how He expects me to do it. That, I have learned, is when faith takes over.

After talking with Briar, I felt God lay it on my heart to help her. And as usual I had no idea how to do it. Virgil and I had only one car, so it wasn't like we had an extra one sitting around we could give away. Nor did we have a pile of extra cash we could use to buy other people cars. So I prayed to God for guidance and clarity on how exactly He wanted me to help Briar.

Before I could do anything, I had to talk the matter over with Virgil. Now, Virgil was a godly husband to me long before I became a godly wife to him, and I wasn't surprised in the least that he agreed to help Briar. That still left us with one big question: How?

We both kept praying for guidance, and quietly I shared Briar's predicament, and God's message to help her, with some of our mutual friends. I also posted a request for donations on our social media page, though I was careful not to use Briar's name. All I wrote was that an anonymous single mother needed help.

Very quickly after my posting, the first offer to help came in. It was, God bless her, from Briar.

Gradually, other offers to donate money began to trickle in. I noticed that most of them were from people who didn't have a lot of money but who loved and cherished Briar—people like Virgil and me. That didn't surprise me, either, because in my experience, it is always the people who have the least who end up giving the most.

After a few weeks, the donations stopped coming in. I sat down and counted what we had. Though so many people had opened up their hearts and given what they could, we were still drastically short of what was needed.

Maybe it *was* time to call Oprah, I wondered to myself.

Instead, I continued to call on God.

"I don't get it," I said to Him one night. "I thought You asked me to help her. Was I wrong?"

Just a few hours later, God answered me.

Right around the time I was feeling I had failed in our mission to help Briar, I got a phone call from a man named Brad Pryor.

Brad is a good friend who is a farmer in town. I met Brad and his wife, Wendy, when I taught their oldest son in school. They are the sweetest, most humble, God-loving people I've ever met. Together with his siblings, parents, and sister-in-law, Brad formed a band called Grace Street Praise Team that travels to different churches in different states leading people in worship. Brad even started his own ministry, Cross Brand Ministries, which began with him helping to feed the local college rodeo team every

Tuesday night. He gave the team members all the food they could want, with only one condition—they had to listen to him talk about God while they ate.

"If you feed them," Brad liked to say, "they will come."

Because of his ministry, several young kids from all over North America have come to find a relationship with the Lord, some for the very first time.

I love how strong and vibrant Brad's faith is, how his devotion to God is so active, so physical, so *alive*. Brad's faith has truly been ignited.

"Crystal, I have to apologize to you," he said when he called me. "I got your email two weeks ago, and God told me back then that I was to help you, but I didn't. If it's okay with you, I'd like to help now."

I told Brad it was more than okay.

Within a week Brad called me back and told me he'd found a car. It belonged to a pastor he knew, and the pastor was willing to sell for a reasonable amount. I told Brad we hadn't raised that much, and thanked him anyway.

"Don't worry about that now," Brad said. "Just tell Briar to come see this car."

A few days later, I invited Briar to our house. She came over with her son, and not long after she arrived, we heard a car pull into our driveway. We went outside, and Brad stepped out of the car.

It was a beautiful black four-door that was shining brightly from a recent washing. All four tires were brand new. It had new tinted windows, new detailing inside, new windshield wipers, and a full tank of gas. Brad had seen to all of that.

I looked at Briar and I saw tears running down her face.

"Here you go," Brad said to her, handing her the keys and an envelope. Inside the envelope was enough money to pay for the car's taxes, title, and insurance.

"This is from the Lord," Brad said.

Briar was beside herself. She ran to Brad and gave him the biggest hug, and then she ran to the car and leaned gently over the front hood and tried to hug the car, too. She got inside and held the steering wheel and tried the power windows and wiped the tears from her eyes.

She wasn't the only one crying.

"Thank you, Lord, oh, thank you, sweet Savior!" Briar said over and over. She pulled her son close to her and said, "Josh, do you see what God can do? Do you see?"

I sidled up to Brad and whispered, "What on earth have you done, Brad Pryor? You know we didn't raise enough to cover this."

"Don't worry about it," Brad said. "It's paid in full. Like I said, it's from the Lord."

Brad was and is the kind of Christian I strive to be. He doesn't just read the words in the Bible—he lives by them every day. He follows up his deep and beautiful faith in God with loving, positive action time and time again. This is only one of many stories I could share about Brad and how he has helped people, most of the time without them ever knowing it was him. That is how he prefers it.

Brad is an angel disguised as a cowboy.

I asked Brad and Briar to pose in front of the car so I could take a picture. I wanted to always remember what Briar's face looked like that day. But when I looked at the photo later, it wasn't Briar's beaming smile that touched my heart the most.

It was Brad's.

The photo I took of Briar and her new car is memorable for another reason. It's memorable because it clearly shows the license plate of the car. It is the same plate that was on the car before Brad got it and fixed it up. When we noticed it, we all laughed, because we all knew just how true it was. It wasn't a coincidence or a fluke—it was a message straight from God.

There on the license plate were two small words.

Love Wins.

CHAPTER EIGHT

Christmas Angels

R IGHT AROUND THE TIME BRIAR GOT HER NEW
car, I began volunteering with a charitable organization in my
town. The group's mission, as stated on their website, is to assist
the needy financially and spiritually by helping with utility bills,
medical prescriptions, food, and things like that.

This mission appealed to me, mainly because for the longest
time I'd been one of those people needing help with *all* those
things.

When I was a single, struggling mother working in a country
bar and taking care of my two young kids, I found myself having
to choose between paying the gas bill or the electricity bill just
about every month. I remember the lights suddenly going off one
night, plunging us into darkness and scaring the kids. I hugged
them close and told them, "It's just a storm, don't be scared, the
lights will come back soon." I understood the sadness and desperation of those who continually fell short of making ends meet,
and I wanted to do what I could to help them.

The director of the group was a passionate woman named Paula. She and I had known each other since we were teens. We'd both hung with the same rough crowd and we'd made several of the same youthful mistakes. And like me, Paula had fought her way out of an early bad marriage. At one point she'd even found herself homeless. Still, she worked tirelessly to provide for her kids, and eventually she remarried. She understood, as well as anyone, what it was like to struggle in your life.

Paula was like me in another way—she'd been unsure of the reality of God. Swarmed by the lies of the enemy, she'd even thought about killing herself, like I had. That was when the Lord reached in and saved her. She felt Him and she heard Him and she accepted Him as her Savior. She became the driving force that ultimately helped lead her husband and children to the Lord, too.

Paula ran the charitable operation out of a plain storefront in our town's downtown area. It was stocked with old office equipment and donated furniture. Families came in for financial assistance with food, utility bills, and other needed services. Counselors sat with the families, talked them through whatever crises were at hand, helped provide resources, and shared the love of the Lord with them. The operation was funded totally by donations and staffed by volunteers.

When I started there, Paula had me sit at the front desk. My job was to greet the families coming in and assess their needs. Family after family poured in, filled out forms, and sat in small plastic chairs, waiting to see a counselor. Each day we'd meet people who had no food, no clothing, and most of the time, no hope. My heart broke for them. Sometimes I'd feel overwhelmed by it all, and I'd slip away to the back of the office and pray.

The week before Christmas, Paula pulled out a big box of

wrapping paper from the closet where she kept donated items. She asked me to help distribute it to the families in the waiting area. I brought the rolls up front and handed them out, and pretty soon nearly all of them were gone.

Then I noticed a woman sitting by herself in the corner of the front office. I went over to her with two rolls of wrapping paper. The woman was blond and skinny, probably in her late thirties or early forties. She'd signed up to speak with a counselor and now she was waiting patiently, looking down, and avoiding eye contact. I smiled and held out the wrapping paper.

"This is all I have left," I told her. "Either blue with snowflakes or red with Santas. Which one would you like?"

Slowly, she looked up at me and said, "Oh, I don't need any."

"Oh, awesome," I said. "You already have your gifts wrapped?"

"No, ma'am," she said. "I don't have any gifts."

"Oh," I said. "Do you have children?"

She nodded and softly said she had a daughter who was three.

I felt just awful. My heart broke for her. Even during my darkest days, I'd always been fortunate enough to be able to get my kids at least one Christmas gift each. They never had an extravagant Christmas or even a normal Christmas when I was a single mom, but they always had something, as humble and modest as it might have been. To not be able to buy even *one* gift had to be excruciating. I walked back to the front desk and put the wrapping paper away.

A few minutes later the woman, whose name was Lori, got called in to see a counselor. Ten minutes later, she was done. I watched her walk out of the office. As she left, I felt a powerful, inexplicable urge to go after her.

So I did.

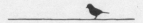

I caught up to her in the parking lot, where it looked like she was waiting for someone to pick her up.

"Excuse me," I said, "I don't mean to intrude, but the dollar store donated some small toys and I have them in my car if you'd like to look at them and maybe pick out something for your little girl."

Lori looked at me and hesitated. I wondered if I'd overstepped a boundary.

Finally she said, "Okay."

I walked toward my car, which was parked nearby. Tentatively, Lori followed. I popped open my trunk, and inside was a little mountain of small toys. Earlier that day, Paula had me pick them up from the local dollar store. The plan was to pass them out at a shelter and a local, low-income school. But now I couldn't help myself. My heart just hurt too much for Lori. I had been her, and I knew her pain, and I wanted her not to feel it anymore, at least for a little while.

"I'm sure there is something in here she may like," I said.

Lori just stood there looking at the pile of toys. Slowly she reached into the trunk and pulled out a tiny doll. Together we picked out a few more gifts for her daughter.

"Now you're gonna need that wrapping paper!" I said, smiling.

Just then Lori's friend arrived to pick her up. Lori showed her the doll and the two other toys she'd picked out. "Look at what this lady gave me," she said.

"Oh no, not me," I said. "I'm just the person in the middle."

I introduced myself to Lori's friend and stuck out my hand.

"I'm Sue," she said.

Sue was different from Lori. She was taller and had a thicker frame. Her red hair hung to her shoulders and she seemed a bit gruff. She didn't smile or try to make conversation. You could almost see life's struggles etched on her face.

I asked Sue if she needed any wrapping paper, since I had one roll left.

"Nah," she said. "I don't get my girls anything until after Christmas, when things are cheaper."

The polite thing for me to do would have been to leave it at that and not ask any follow-up questions. This wasn't my job. My job was handing out wrapping paper, not prying into people's personal lives. But that had never stopped me before, so why start then?

"You mean you don't have anything for your girls for Christmas?" I asked.

Sue's head cocked to the side and she gave me a harsh look that said, "What part of what I just said did you not understand, lady?"

What happened next happened quickly. So quickly that I didn't have a chance to think about it. Instead I just blurted it out, as if it were someone else's idea.

"Can I take you guys Christmas shopping on Saturday?" I asked.

Lori and Sue looked at each other, then looked back at me.

"What?" they both asked, almost in unison.

It was the same question I was screaming to myself in my head—*Crystal, what on earth are you doing?* But even though I was as confused as they were, I did what I usually do—I kept talking.

"I don't have much, but I do have two hundred dollars," I said, referring to what was left in my family's Christmas budget. "We can find a few things for your girls. I'm not crazy, I promise. If you want, I can give you my phone number and you can think about it and maybe call me and we can set something up for this Saturday."

Another uncomfortable silence followed, until finally Sue said, "Are you being serious right now?"

I nodded and told her I was. But in own mind, I was asking myself the same thing.

"Why would you do something like that for us?" Sue asked. "You don't even know us."

"Because I know what it feels like to struggle during the holiday season as a single mom," I said.

Sue looked at me hard. I'm sure she was trying to figure out just when I'd lost my mind. But as she stared at me, I noticed something—the very, very beginning of a tear in her eye.

"Well, yeah," Sue said sheepishly, "that would be really nice."

I scribbled my number on a piece of paper and handed it to Sue. Just as I did, Lori lunged at me and hugged me so tight you'd have thought I'd just handed her a million dollars. Since I'd already clearly overstepped, I decided, what the heck? I grabbed Sue and pulled her into our hug and we all squeezed each other tight. What can I say? I'm a hugger who has problems with boundaries sometimes.

Later, I prayed and thanked God for bringing these women to that parking lot that day. It felt like we became a band of sisters in that moment, but I also understood, as I walked back to the office, that we might never see each other again.

My next thought was that I probably should have run my little idea past Virgil first. The reason I didn't was because I already knew what he would say. Convincing him to donate money we didn't really have was always the easy part. Convincing myself was the real battle. But this time, even I hadn't struggled with the decision. It was just very clear to me that this was something I needed to do.

"Well, you're going to have to fire me," I said to Paula when I found her in the back of the office. "I think I just broke all your rules."

I told her about Sue and Lori and the toys in the trunk and our Saturday shopping trip, and Paula looked at me and shook her head and smiled.

"That's all on you, love," she said. "Now get back to work."

That evening, I shared my little mission on Facebook, and without naming names I wrote about the two sweet women who Santa seemed to have forgotten. I didn't expect much of a response—after all, most people were busy with their own Christmas shopping—but within twenty minutes, four different friends came by my house to drop off toys and money. I even got a message from an old high school friend of mine, Jane.

Jane and I had been part of the same crowd in high school, and let's just say Jane could vouch for the kind of wild situations I got myself into back then. We both had our share of issues to deal with and we both wound up dropping out of high school and going to an alternative school. Eventually, we both became teenage single mothers. I like to think of us as good girls who occasionally did bad things. Even so, we both pulled ourselves out of our messes, finished college, and created pretty good lives for ourselves.

We hadn't spoken in a while, so I was surprised and happy to get a message from her.

"I work for JCPenney now," Jane wrote, describing her job orchestrating photo shoots and designing layouts for the store's catalogs. "I've got some JCPenney gift certificates you can use, and I'll also tell the manager at the store that you're coming.

"I remember being where these women are," Jane also wrote. "I remember how rough it was."

You and me both, sister, I thought.

My doorbell rang nonstop that night as people continued to bring their love offerings. By the time Saturday rolled around, my original two-hundred-dollar donation had nearly tripled.

Sue did indeed call me the next day, and we arranged to meet outside JCPenney on Saturday morning. Virgil came along to give us a hand. Lori was late, so we went in without her.

I could tell Sue was nervous about the whole thing. She didn't know me and she didn't know why I was doing this, and her defenses were clearly up. For all she knew I was some rich woman taking pity on her. I hadn't told her about my time in heaven or about how God had changed my life—and I wasn't sure I was going to.

"So what do you want to look at first?" I asked her.

"Well, my girls really need pants," she said.

We went to the clothing department and Sue waded through the stacks of pants, comparing prices. She'd find a pair that she liked, look at the price, and put it back. That's when I decided to tell her that on top of the $100 we'd promised her, we had gift certificates for her for another $150.

"Really?" she said quietly. "Wow. Just, wow."

"I know! Isn't God so good?" I said, smiling a huge, cheesy smile.

Sue looked at me and walked away without saying a word.

We kept shopping and I didn't bring up God again. Instead, we traded stories about our daughters. Bit by bit, I felt Sue's defenses lowering. Then, as we rummaged through the clearance rack, all the electrical power in the store suddenly went out. An employee made an announcement letting us know the outage would be fixed soon. It was too dark to keep shopping, so Sue and I sat down in the middle of the aisle and talked.

"This reminds me of my life as a single mother," I said. "My power would go out all the time."

Sue laughed and told me about her own struggles with money and with men. Everything she described was familiar to me from my old life—the loneliness, the panic, the feeling that God had abandoned her. I wanted to tell her God had not abandoned her, and I wanted to tell her how I knew that, but I held my tongue. I didn't think that Sue was ready to hear about how much God loved her, because she couldn't see the evidence of that in her difficult life.

No one understood that better than I did.

When we sat on the floor together, I noticed Sue's shoes. They were old white tennis shoes, and they were falling apart. I could see her toes through the holes.

"You ought to get yourself some new shoes while you're here," I said.

"Oh no," Sue said. "This is just for my girls. It's all for my girls."

Eventually the power in the store came back on, and we returned to shopping. Lori showed up a bit later, and when she did I also told her about the extra money she had to spend. The three of us approached a store manager so I could find out how to use the gift certificates my friend Jane gave us. The manager, a polite, pleasant-looking man in his thirties, looked at me kind of strangely and asked, "Are you Crystal?"

"Yes," I said.

"Jane's friend?"

"Yes, that's right."

"Hold on just a second," he said. Then he disappeared.

Bad thoughts raced through my mind. Had Jane done something wrong by giving us the gift certificates? Was he going to refuse to allow us to use them? A few minutes later, the manager came back. Two young, smiling women were with him, and he was carrying something in his arms that totally confused me.

He was carrying two gigantic bouquets of roses.

"I understand we have two very special customers here today," the manager said.

The manager handed one bouquet to Sue and the other to Lori. They accepted the roses with baffled smiles. Sue, who up until then had been so hard and so shut off, couldn't help tearing up with emotion.

"Oh my gosh," she said. "I've never been given flowers before in my life."

The manager also gave each of them a Christmas card with more gift certificates and discount coupons inside.

"These young ladies are your personal shoppers," he explained to them. "They will help you with anything you need. Are you hungry or thirsty? Can we get you anything?"

We spent the next two hours shopping and smiling and laughing. Lori's personal shopper helped her pick out dresses and jackets for her three-year-old daughter, while I finally persuaded Sue to get a new pair of shoes for herself. The discount coupons the manager gave us just about doubled the amount Sue and Lori could spend. When we finally had everything we needed, Virgil and I helped the ladies carry their bags and flowers to the parking lot. We reached Sue's car, and Sue came toward me and wrapped me in a big hug.

"I don't know what to say," she said. "I don't know how to thank you."

"This isn't from me," I said. "This is all from God. God loves you and He loves your girls. I know this, because He once showed me how much He loves me."

Virgil and I helped them load up their car, and we watched them drive away.

I got in our car and I asked Virgil not to drive just yet. Then I cried for five minutes while Virgil waited patiently for me to finish. He understood why I was crying. I was overwhelmed by how my community responded to the needs of these women, and I was overwhelmed by how much pride and strength Sue and Lori had shown. Most of all, I was overwhelmed by what God had done.

Here I'd been, nervous about giving my own money to these women, feeling like I was out on a limb all by myself, doing something crazy.

But God had much bigger plans for Sue and Lori than I'd ever dreamed of! God multiplied the blessing! And no, I *hadn't* been alone through this—not even close. In the end, somewhere around thirty other people got involved in the

Christmas miracle. A small army, to be sure, but an army nonetheless.

Finally, I told Virgil I was done crying, and we drove to Walmart and finished our own Christmas shopping.

That night I got a phone call.

"Is this Crystal?" the lady on the other end asked.

"Yes."

"Crystal McVea?"

"Yes," I said, thinking, *Oh great, a bill collector.*

Then the lady said, "The woman you took shopping today was my daughter."

It was Sue's mother. She explained how Sue had called her and told her everything—about the gift certificates, the discount coupons, the beautiful roses, the presents, and the shoes. "It was like I was a contestant in a beauty pageant!" Sue had said.

"She has been through so many hard times, and she works so hard, and I am just so thankful to you for allowing this to happen," her mother told me. "Sue has a big heart, but it's been broken so many times. She just lost her brother to cancer this past October. She moved him into her house and took care of him to the very end. She is such a hard worker and she helps so many people, but she doesn't let many people into her world. I can't thank you enough for what you did today."

"Well, it wasn't me at all," I said through my own tears. "It was all God."

"Yes, that's what Sue said, too. She said she couldn't believe God would do all this for her and her daughters."

When I went to bed that night I said a prayer and lay in awe of God's work. I marveled at how He had broken through Sue's defenses simply by showing her she was valuable and loved. I had been longing for heaven from the moment I came back to earth, and that night I realized I had seen a glimpse of heaven again, here on earth.

Who knew I would see it in a JCPenney store?

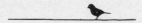

CHAPTER NINE

Stone Soup

MY TIME IN HEAVEN GAVE ME AN URGENCY TO do something for God.

But it was my experiences with Briar, Sue, and Lori that began to teach me what that "something" could be.

It reminds me of the old folk tale "Stone Soup."

A group of travelers arrives at a village with no food and only a cooking pot. At first, no one in the village is willing to share their food with the group. Then the travelers fill their pot with water, put it over a fire, and drop a stone in it. Suddenly, the villagers are curious.

"We're making stone soup," one traveler explains. "All it needs is a little garnishing to make it taste even better."

One villager, no longer worried that he has to feed the whole group, happily hands over a carrot. Another hands over some celery. Another delivers several spices. Before long all the villagers have contributed something, and they all enjoy the nourishing soup together.

This is how each and every one of us can experience the thrill of chasing heaven on earth—by contributing *something*.

It wasn't me who got the car for Briar. And it wasn't me who gave Sue and Lori roses and extra coupons. In both cases, all I did was get the ball rolling. In the end, lots of different people had a big hand in changing the lives of these women.

And it happened only because everyone *played their part*.

Maybe it's baking cookies for a fund-raiser. Maybe it's writing a hopeful note for someone who is struggling. Maybe it's simply blocking out ten minutes to *pray* for someone who needs our help. God chooses different roles for different people.

And if a whole bunch of different people hadn't played their parts, what happened with Briar and Sue and Lori might not have happened at all.

We might have just ended up with a stone and an empty pot.

This is what dying taught me about living—that we all have a part to play, and that no part is too small. We must open our eyes and pay attention to what part we can play each day in the service of God.

So look around you. See where you're needed. Do what you can. Play your part. Because if we all chase heaven in our own way, through us, God will nourish the world.

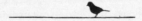

CHAPTER TEN

All Dogs Go to Heaven

THE DAY I DIED, MY TWINS, MICAH AND WILLOW, were barely ten months old. Three years later, when my book *Waking Up in Heaven* came out, they were still too young to understand much of what had happened to me.

But unlike my older two children, the twins grew up with a mom who talked about God and heaven constantly. I never shied away from discussing my experience around them, though I was careful about how much I revealed. The twins loved watching YouTube videos of me talking about heaven, and they loved taking a magazine that featured our story to school for show-and-tell. Mainly, I suspected, so they could just show their friends how they were in the magazine, too.

Still, like most kids, the idea of dying was scary to them. When I talked about what happened to me, I tried my best to describe my experience on a level they could understand. Mainly, I wanted them to know that God was real and that He loved them very much. On top of our usual prayers at home, I would often pray with the twins in the car on the way to the school bus stop.

"Okay, who wants to lead the prayer this morning?" I'd ask.

And Willow would say, "God, I hope You have a great day today."

At night we'd pray again before bed. One evening, Micah was clamoring for a bedtime snack, and I had to be stern with him and tell him it was time for prayers and bed.

"Dear Lord," I began, "we pray for all of the children who are hungry."

"*But I hungry!*" Micah interrupted. "*I hungry!*"

Another time, after our family came back home from a trip to Disney World, Micah realized we'd left his favorite stuffed monkey behind. He was devastated. The hotel never found it, so I found another monkey that looked the same online, and I had it mailed to us. One day, Micah included his lost monkey in his prayers. That evening, he accompanied me to the mailbox, where, low and behold, the monkey sat. It was a miracle—his prayer had been answered.

That's when Willow ran inside and said, "I'm going to pray for a unicorn!"

Which led to a discussion about how God answers all our prayers, but sometimes the answer is no.

Many evenings I'd sit on the children's beds and watch Virgil tell them stories about the Lord and read to them from their children's Bibles. We wanted the twins to know that God is real— that He is someone they can have an actual relationship with.

"But I can't see Him," Willow once said.

"Well, we can't see the wind, but we can feel it and we know it's real," I said. "It's the same with God."

Virgil and I also took the twins along on many of our mission outreaches. We wanted them to see up close what it meant to put your faith into action. The twins quietly soaked it all up like sponges, and by the time they were five I could tell they were thoughtful, compassionate kids. Best of all, I could tell they were developing their own relationships with God. They loved Him with a purity that I prayed would stay with them as they grew up.

Sometimes we'll say, "Oh, kids, they don't understand," but I think that often kids understand things even better than we do. I think we can learn a lot from the way our children love so innocently and unconditionally. I know I learn valuable lessons from my children all the time.

One evening, I got a call from my girlfriend Christie. Her voice sounded frantic.

"Is Virgil home?" she asked.

"Christie, what's wrong?"

"It's Roscoe," she said.

Christie was the mother of three young boys, and she was raising them by herself while her husband, who was in the military, was deployed overseas for a full year. I'd bring the twins over for playdates, and my kids particularly loved playing with Christie's big, friendly yellow Labrador retriever, Roscoe. Roscoe was a solid hundred pounds and around seventeen years old, but he loved children and he let them hug on him all day long. My kids came to love Roscoe like he was their own dog.

"He can't move," Christie told me through tears. "He tries to get up and he keeps falling down. I need to take him to the vet but I can't lift him."

Virgil and I took the twins and drove to Christie's house. Virgil went inside and carried Roscoe out to Christie's van. Once Roscoe was as comfortable as they could make him, Virgil drove the twins home and I went with Christie to the vet's office. At one point Christie got up and moved three feet away to fill out some forms. Poor Roscoe started trying to drag himself toward her, whimpering. My heart just broke in half. Christie put the forms down and hugged Roscoe and didn't let go.

Christie slowly nodded as the vet explained what we both already understood. Roscoe was old, and it was his time. I stayed with Christie while she said her good-byes. She never stopped hugging and holding her sweet friend until he took his last breath.

That evening I sat down with the twins to explain to them what had happened.

"Roscoe was very sick and very old," I told them, "and he went to heaven to be with God."

"Did he die?" Willow asked.

I nodded.

With that, she and Micah went back to playing with blocks on the floor. Neither said another word about Roscoe.

The next day, Willow came bounding up to me and said, "Mommy, can we go to Christie's and see Roscoe?"

"No, baby, remember, he went to heaven," I told her as I stroked her hair. I was preparing for a fallout of emotions from her, but it never came.

A few days later Willow asked me, "Mommy, when is Roscoe coming back?"

"What do you mean, baby?"

"You know, when will God send Roscoe back from heaven?"

That's when it dawned on me—Willow believed *everyone* who dies and goes to heaven comes back.

Why wouldn't she believe that? After all, the only person she knew who had died had in fact come back, so why not Roscoe? I called Micah over, and once again sat down with the twins.

"I want to explain something," I said. "The doctors were able to help me come back from heaven. But most people and most animals that die don't come back. They are so lucky and they get to stay in heaven."

I couldn't be sure how much of this they understood. All by itself, death is a pretty heavy concept, and it takes most of us many, many years to come to a real understanding of our mortality. Now throw in the idea that some people get to come back, and it gets even more complicated. I encouraged the twins to come to me with any questions they might have, even though I knew I didn't have all the answers. In heaven, I had no questions for God because all knowledge was given to me in that moment. But back here on earth, in this life, I had not been allowed to retain all that God had told me. That left me with plenty of questions of my own.

In the five years since I returned from heaven, however, my understanding of my time there has changed. Just as the lessons I learned in heaven have helped me live a better life on earth, my experiences here during those five years have helped illuminate my understanding of heaven.

For one thing, people have pointed out to me that I was not in fact in heaven because I did not pass through the gates. The truth is, I never actually even saw gates—what I saw was a brilliant profusion of love and life dancing together and beckoning me to come closer. And I understood that if I walked into this light, I would be in my forever home. And even though I didn't walk into the light, I still call the place where I was "heaven." I call it heaven because I don't know what else I could call it. To me, being with my angels and with God, and being wrapped in such incredible love, was, in fact, heaven.

When I returned, I was delighted to learn I was not the only person who had experienced this majestic place. Don Piper, the pastor who was dead for an hour and a half before being revived, talks about it in his book *90 Minutes in Heaven*. He, too, made it through the tunnel and right up to the gates, but like me he didn't pass through them. And like me he understood that if he had passed through the gates, he wouldn't have been able to come back to earth.

Why do some people go up to the gates but not pass through?

In the five years since I've been back, I've come to understand that God uses us all in different ways. He has a *purpose* for us that is specific to who we are. My purpose, and Don's purpose, involved coming back to earth. But others are permitted to enter those beautiful gates and run into the arms of the Lord. When someone we love dies, it is painful beyond words, but only for us, not them. The truth is, we are not really losing them—and one day we will see them again.

I believe this is why God sends some people back—to share the message that heaven is real and He loves us and He is waiting for us in our final home.

At the same time, God wants us to live full and joyful lives right here, right now. Our time on earth is as much a part of our journey as our time in heaven. The love we create and share here matters—it matters *greatly*. As beautiful and desirable as heaven is, I wouldn't have wanted to miss any of the life I've lived here.

Heaven is real, but so is our life on earth—and they are both a part of God's exquisite and perfect plan for each of us.

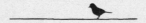

CHAPTER ELEVEN

Touching Heaven

I HAD ALWAYS BEEN TERRIFIED OF DYING. FROM the time I was a little girl, the thought of what suffering might await me, plus my fear of the unknown, filled me with dread. To me, death seemed cruel, random, and horrible. I was seven when I lost my beloved grandmother, Ernie, and when she passed away, I lashed out at God.

"I hate You! I hate You! I hate You!" I screamed.

Death was my worst nightmare, until I experienced it for myself.

In heaven, God allowed me a glimpse of what happens when we leave our lives on earth, and He showed me that the transition is not only painless but also glorious. Even more profoundly, in heaven I gained the knowledge that we never truly die. Our spirits continue on. Standing at those gates of heaven with God, I was more alive than I had ever been before. "I am the resurrection and the life," the Lord said in John 11:25. "The one who believes in Me will live, even though they die."

One of the most extraordinary things God allowed me to do upon my return was to share my story of heaven with people who would soon be experiencing it themselves.

In *Waking Up in Heaven*, I told the story of Danny. Danny was a young pastor who lived a few towns away from me. He had a beautiful wife, Danica, and a precious family. God used Danny and Danica to minister to my family the year my twins were born prematurely. Just a few months after I died, we heard Danny had terminal cancer. In the final days of his life, he told his wife he wanted to talk with me.

I called Danica and arranged a time for Virgil, my mother, and I to go over and sit with Danny. We found him in a hospital bed set up in the living room. I pulled up a chair and took Danny's hand. Before his illness, he'd been incredibly fit and robust, but now he was frail and thin. I felt him squeeze my hand as he turned to look at me. A slight smile formed on his face. Before I could say anything, Danny spoke.

"Tell me about heaven," he said. "Tell me what it's going to be like to die."

So I told him everything. I told him about dying and waking up in heaven, my angels, the little girl with the golden basket, the long tunnel, and of course, being with God. Two weeks after our talk, Pastor Danny traveled down the same beautiful tunnel of light that I remembered so vividly, and through the gates of heaven, into the arms of the Lord.

My time with Danny changed me so much. He inspired me to continue talking about heaven. Because of Danny, I was ready a few months later when the makeup artist asked me about my time in heaven before my appearance on *Fox & Friends*. Because I had feared death for most of my life, I understood how scared people who were seriously ill could be. And I came to learn that one of the most divine and heartbreaking parts of life happens when you share yourself with those who are getting ready to leave it.

During my moment of vulnerability after the *Fox & Friends* segment, one woman's kind words in an email showed me that God finds a way to speak to me—even back here on earth. Peggy had sent the email to me sharing that God had instructed her to pray for me. Amid the harsh and painful words from faceless Internet bullies that day, when I read Peggy's email, her love and support just washed over me. We became friends, and I came to learn that Peggy is a nurse, and her husband is the CEO of their local hospital. She was involved in organizing a women's conference, and she wanted me to come and address the five hundred or so women who were attending.

Just the thought of speaking in front of so many people made me feel sick. I love to talk, but at the same time, *public* speaking makes me very nervous. I truly hate the idea of a roomful of people staring at me and waiting for me to say something. Visualizing myself in front of all those women made my stomach curl in knots. But by then I knew I couldn't be guided by my fears. God told me to tell people what I could remember, and that was exactly what I was going to do. So I told Peggy I'd be honored to speak at the conference.

I wanted Virgil to come with me, but he couldn't attend because of work. So my sweet friend Kelli came instead. The conference was in a town right along the Texas-Mexico border. Because of the drug wars across the border, Virgil was worried about my safety. Recently, the U.S. government had instructed all its employees not to go into Mexico.

"Under no circumstances do you go anywhere near the border," Virgil warned me. "And don't get into cars with people you don't know."

"Of course I won't," I assured my husband.

I thought of that promise a few days later as I headed to the border in a stranger's car.

In my defense, I didn't really have much choice. After I gave my speech at the conference, a woman came up to me near the front of the room. Her face was red from crying. She approached me shyly and hesitated before speaking.

"This is a long shot, I know," she finally said, "but one of my best friends is dying. She has two kids and she doesn't have much time left. And I was wondering . . ."

"Let's go," I said without hesitation.

"What?" she said. "Really?"

"Yes, let's go."

I got into a car with a small group of people—a local pastor and his wife, one of the worship leaders at the conference, and the woman whose friend was dying—and we drove to her friend's home.

Which happened to be right on the Mexican border.

The ailing woman, Maria, was in her forties, and she was nearing the end of her battle with cancer. A large tumor in her brain had left her unable to speak, though her family told us she could understand what was happening around her and would try to communicate in writing when she was able. Maria lay in a hospital bed in a tiny bedroom at the back of the modest house. We squeezed around her bedside, twenty of us in all, including her family. As a man began to gently play his guitar, I worked my way to this woman's bedside and took her hand in mine. The room filled with the sounds of worship being sung in Spanish. I didn't need to understand the words to feel the love and praise being laid at the feet of the Lord in that room.

After a few more songs and some prayer, a family member told Maria who I was and where I had been. Then they translated for her as I began to share with her what I experienced in heaven. I told her about my angels and about the beauty of the tunnel. I explained to her about how loving and almighty God is. I told her that in the moment I died, there was no pain or fear. I leaned over and whispered in her ear, "You don't have to be afraid."

Out of the corner of my eye I saw two teenage children wiping away tears. I knew right away they were Maria's children, and I knew she had to be afraid for them, more than she was for herself.

"God showed me something in heaven," I told her. "He showed me that my children would be okay without me. You do not have to be afraid. God will take care of them."

And then I felt it—the woman's thin, bony hand squeezing mine.

I leaned forward and kissed her gently on the forehead. Then I whispered in her ear again.

"I will meet you there someday," I said, "right at the gates. We'll talk about how beautiful it all is."

A few months later, I heard through friends that a woman in my hometown, Christie, wanted me to speak with her dying husband, Kenneth. He was in the final stages of his battle with cancer, and they both knew his time left on earth was short.

Virgil and I took the twins and drove over to their home, and Christie greeted us at the front door. We all hugged, and Christie led us into the living room, where Kenneth was resting in his recliner. Christie offered the twins some snacks and they soon disappeared to play with Virgil in another room.

Kenneth was in his pajamas, with a blanket pulled over him, his eyes closed. He was a tall man but very thin, and my first thought was that he looked familiar. I sat on the sofa, beside his chair.

"Hello, Mr. Lemaster, my name's Crystal."

"Hello, Crystal," Kenneth said. "Please excuse me; I have to keep my eyes shut. I can't focus very well anymore."

"That is not a problem, sir," I said as I scooted down to the end of the couch to be closer to him. "I just want to say how very sorry I am that you have to go through all of this right now. I wish I had some words that could make it go away."

Kenneth smiled, and Christie went into the kitchen to get us some refreshments. Kenneth explained how very grateful he was for his wife, and how she basically never left his side. He told me he felt guilty that she had to care for him in such a way.

"I know I am dying," Kenneth said, "but my love for her will never, ever die."

I felt myself choke up with emotion. I knew what that kind of love felt like.

"Kenneth, how can I help you the most right now, friend?" I asked.

He paused for a moment and cleared his throat.

"I know where I am going," he said. "But I've never been there and I want to know what it's going to be like when the time comes."

I shared everything I could about heaven. Only once did Kenneth interrupt me.

"Angels?" he asked.

"Yes," I said. "They were there with me from the moment I arrived, and they showed me they are with us always. They are here with you right now, but it is only when we pass that the veil is opened and we can see clearly that we were never alone."

With these words, Kenneth began to cry. His wife, Christie, was crying, too, and she leaned in and told me why.

"That is my greatest fear," she said. "That Ken will be all alone. I don't want him to be all alone."

"He won't be, not ever," I said. "Not for one single second."

We all sat together in the living room sharing, crying, and laughing for about forty-five special minutes. Finally, after racking my brain to figure out why Kenneth looked so familiar, I finally said, "I know you somehow."

But before he could respond, it dawned on me.

"Oh my gosh," I said. "Did you once work for the sheriff's office?"

"Yes, I sure did," Kenneth said.

"That's how I know you!" I said. "You arrested me once!"

Kenneth laughed and said, "Surely it wasn't me, Crystal."

Then I told him the story of one of the worst days of my life.

Long ago, long before I went to heaven, I was pulled over by the police and given a warning for not having my insurance verification. I was late for work and my kids were yelling and crying in the backseat. As a result, I didn't hear the police officer explaining that I needed to provide proof of insurance within a certain number of days to avoid further consequences.

Six months later, those consequences came. I was a divorced, single mother of two young kids, and I was putting myself through college. My ex-husband had a warrant out for his arrest because he owed me child support. Finally, I'd had enough of being the only financial supporter for my children, and went to the sheriff's department to turn in my ex-husband. A tall cowboy dressed in his sheriff's uniform greeted me at the front desk. I explained my situation, and he ran my ex's name through the computer. For some reason, nothing came up. I leaned over to look at the computer monitor and noticed my own name on the screen.

"Right there!" I said. "That's my name! Could his warrant be tied to my name since he owes me money?"

The officer looked at the screen and looked back at me.

"This is you?" he asked. "Crystal?"

"Yes, that's me."

"Well, Crystal," he said, "I'm afraid you are under arrest."

All I could say in return was, "Uh, excuse me?"

The officer placed handcuffs on my wrists and said, "Honey, you have the right to remain silent." Naturally, I immediately waived that right because there was no way I could stay silent.

"I don't even know what I did wrong," I said through tears.

It turned out there was a warrant for my arrest because I'd never gone back to court to show proof of my car insurance.

My heart sank all the way to the floor. My children were both in day care, and I had to go pick them up in a matter of hours. This couldn't be happening.

"How long will I be arrested for?" I asked the officer.

"Well, ya gotta make bail and then appear in court," he said kindly but matter-of-factly.

A different officer took me to a back room for my fingerprints and mug shot. I remember I smiled for the picture, even though I was crying. Suddenly, I felt very angry about my predicament.

"My ex-husband isn't paying child support and I get arrested!" I yelled out.

"Hey, girl, if you don't calm down, I'll have to put you back there," the officer said, motioning up to a screen where I could see a live feed of the jail cells.

I piped down and quietly wept. I was genuinely terrified. I was under arrest, and I was going to jail. I wouldn't be able to pick up my kids from day care. The officer asked me if I wanted to call my parents, and I violently shook my head. There was no way I was going to call my parents. It was somewhere around that time, with the clock ticking toward when my kids got out of day care and me sitting slumped in a chair, crying and sniveling, that the officer came over and sat down next to me.

"Tell you what," he said in a soft voice. "I'll help you make your bail."

He got on the phone and called a local bondsman, who came over to the sheriff's station. My bail was $250, and I pulled out my checkbook to write the check.

"No checks," the bail bondsman said.

"Go ahead and take her check," the officer told him. "I'll vouch for her and I'll personally take her to court."

The bail bondsman agreed, and the officer walked me out of the station and to the courthouse one block over. I was in handcuffs, and I prayed no one who knew me would see me. At the courthouse I started crying even harder, and the sheriff kept talking to me in a low, even voice, trying to calm me down.

"Crystal, are you hungry?" he asked. I shook my head no but thanked him anyway. Then he reached over and took off my handcuffs.

"I may be a big boy, but I can still run pretty fast," he warned me with a smile. I smiled back and rubbed my sore wrists. We sat and talked for what seemed like a long, long time.

Then it was time for me to see the judge. When I heard my name, I stood up and my legs were shaking so badly I was afraid I might fall over. The bigger fear, though, was that I might start laughing hysterically, as I sometimes do in stressful situations.

The judge looked over the rim of her glasses and directly at me.

"You cannot run from your responsibilities," she said. "You cannot simply refuse to obey the laws without consequences. Do you understand?"

I nodded in acknowledgment.

"Your Honor," the officer began, "this young lady actually turned herself in today."

Yeah, I thought, *he's right*. Only I was stupid enough to accidentally turn myself in!

I pled guilty and I was given a fine. The judge called someone else's name, and I turned and went back to the officer.

"You're free to go now," he said. "See, that wasn't so bad."

He walked me back to my car and watched as I slid into the driver's seat.

"Just be sure to stay out of trouble," he said. "Now go get your kids."

I made it to the day care with about five minutes to spare.

The officer's name was Kenneth, and he was an angel disguised as a sheriff.

Now, nearly fifteen years later, I found myself across from that sheriff again.

"You have no idea what you did for me that day," I told Kenneth. "You went out of your way to be kind to me. You held my hand through one of the toughest days of my life."

Kenneth smiled warmly and said, "Now you're holding my hand through one of the toughest days of mine."

For a long time I wasn't sure why God sent me back from heaven. But it was becoming clear to me that one of the reasons was to share my experience of heaven with people who are nearing the end of their lives on earth.

We are all human, and even the most faithful among us might feel alone and afraid as we prepare to meet our Creator. Just the act of talking about heaven—of affirming its existence and imagining its glories—can ease those fears and bring some measure of comfort in that time. I was beginning to realize that was something I could help with, because, after all, I *loved* talking about heaven. I would probably do it 24/7 if I could. That God would use me in some small way to help bring solace to those who needed it was incredibly humbling. It filled me with a sense of purpose, as well as a sense of awe at how God uses us all in different ways to share His love with the world.

Virgil and I, along with our friend Brad, went back to see Kenneth and his wife a few days later. Kenneth's condition was deteriorating quickly.

"I know I am getting worse," he told me that day, "but I'm still praying for healing."

"Then I will pray for healing, too," I said. "We will pray for healing until God gives His final answer."

We sat with Kenneth, talking and praying. After a while we got up to leave, but before I left, Kenneth called me to his side.

"I remember what you told me," he whispered. "It won't hurt. And I won't be alone."

"No," I said. "You will be with your angels and with the Lord. Never alone."

Two days later, my friend got to meet his angels face-to-face.

My time with Kenneth—like my time with the makeup artist and the woman in Texas and Pastor Danny—taught me incredible lessons about the role of angels in our lives. In heaven, I was never alone because my angels were there the instant I opened my eyes.

In the same way, we are never alone on earth because we have angels here, too. Some look like cabdrivers, others like cowboys, others like men with badges.

Today, whenever I sit at the bedside of the dying, I picture Kenneth and Danny sitting next to me, guiding me through it. They were my angels during some difficult times on earth, and they are my angels still. Forever connected and never forgotten.

The truth is, I don't know why some people get cancer and die, and others don't. But what I do know, and what I can say for sure, is that God knows our sadness. God knows every single one of our tears. "You keep track of all my sorrows," the psalmist in

56:8 wrote. "You have collected all my tears in your bottle. You have recorded each one in your book" (NLT).

God is there with us in our suffering, and one day He will take it all away.

"He will wipe every tear from their eyes. There will be no more death or mourning or crying or pain," it says in Revelation 21:4. "All these things will be gone forever."

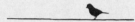

CHAPTER TWELVE

Standing in the Yes

I BELIEVE THAT GOD PERFORMS MIRACLES. BUT WHEN is it right to pray for a miracle, and when is it time for us to let go?

My time in heaven taught me about the incredible power of prayer and about how God is always listening when we ask for miracles. But in the five years since I've been back on earth, I've learned even more about prayer and miracles—through my really good friend Kelly Lieter.

No one loves God quite as joyously as Kelly. She talks about Him all the time, and when she does, she often jumps up and down with excitement. I met Kelly a few years before I died, during a time when my faith was at its lowest point. It was Kelly's passion for God that first caught my attention, but it was her strength and her testimony—a story of loss, hope, and heaven— that eventually caught my heart.

One morning in May 2000, Kelly said good-bye to her son Jonathan, a high school sophomore, as he left the house. Just minutes later, her then-husband called to tell her Jonathan had been in a car wreck just a quarter of a mile from home. When Kelly drove to the scene of the wreck she saw her son lying on the street; he'd been thrown from his car.

"That's my child!" Kelly screamed as she tried to push past a highway patrolman and get to her son. "Is he okay?!"

"We are helping him," is all the patrolman would say.

At the hospital Kelly begged a doctor she knew to check on her son and see if he was okay. "An unfamiliar look came over his face," Kelly recalls. "A look I had never seen before."

"Kelly," the doctor said, "Jonathan didn't make it."

She pushed in to see her son in the emergency room. "His clothes were dirty. His hands were still. His braces showed through his slightly open mouth. He looked okay to me. He had a small cut above his eye, but dead? Really? I laid my head on his chest, which was painfully still. I put my hand on his face. He felt fine. He didn't feel dead. He couldn't be."

A little over two months later, Kelly had a dream. In the dream, she saw Jonathan. "His hair was lighter, longer, free-flowing, and he didn't have his braces. I grabbed him and asked him if he was here to stay. 'Are you alive?' I asked. 'No,' he said, 'not like you.'"

In the dream, Jonathan told his mother what had happened. He'd unhooked his seat belt to reach for a CD he dropped and lost control of the car. "He told me a male nurse came over to him and held his head in his hands, turning his head periodically and saying, 'Come on, kid, you can make it.'"

When the beautiful dream was over, Kelly wondered why no one had mentioned a male nurse to her. She put up a note in the hospital that said, "My son Jonathan died in a car accident north of town. If you are the one who came and stayed by him, please call me." A few weeks later, someone called. It was the male nurse.

He told Kelly he'd been driving home from his shift at the hospital when he saw a red car veer off the road, hit something, and go airborne. He saw Jonathan ejected from the car. He ran over and held her son's head and—just as Jonathan described it in the dream—turned his head to the side a few times. He did it because Jonathan's mouth was filling with blood.

This confirmation that her dream had been real—that her son's spirit had truly come to be with her—led Kelly to beg God to keep her son's spirit close to her forever. But God told her Jonathan's spirit wasn't meant to be confined. It was meant to soar.

"Okay, God, I let him go," Kelly said. "I want him to fly."

It wasn't a hard decision. "It was no longer a struggle," Kelly says. "I didn't even have to try to let him go; it just happened. I wanted his spirit to be free. And when people ask me how I made it through my son's death, my answer is simple: God's grace is all I need."

Not long ago, Kelly called me crying uncontrollably.

"Crystal, I yelled at God tonight," she said between sobs. "I yelled at Him and I said, 'Are You even listening to me? Do my prayers even matter? Or are You just going to do whatever You want anyway?'"

I understood those questions. I had asked them many times myself. But coming from Kelly, they were a surprise. I soon found out why she was questioning God.

Kelly has a friend named Allan Johnson. Allan is a motivational speaker for teachers, and people who know him say he is one of the warmest and most charismatic people they've ever met. Allan calls everyone "friend," even if he's never met them. He is the father of three young children, and he records his own original Gospel music. I had never met Allan, but hearing about him made me feel like I knew him.

Kelly told me how Allan had gone along with some students on a field trip to an amusement park the day before. All of a sudden he slowly crumpled to the ground. He wasn't breathing, and someone began administering CPR. By the time paramedics took him to the hospital, Allan had been without oxygen for what was likely a long while.

At the hospital, the news wasn't good. The doctors believed Allan suffered brain damage and was now "experiencing seizures and unable to awaken," his mother and sister wrote in a blog they started after Allan's collapse. "We continue to ask the Lord for a miracle." When Kelly heard about what happened, she immediately began praying and asking all her friends to pray.

When she called me, she asked if I could come up to see Allan in the hospital. "God is telling me He wants you and Virgil here," she said. The next day we got to the hospital and sat with Allan's mother, Frankye, and his sister, Michelle, in the waiting room.

"They are not giving us much hope," Frankye told me. "They believe that his brain may have been too damaged."

I could see the pain in her eyes and hear it in her voice, and I searched my brain for what to say. Honestly, I wasn't even sure if I was the right person for her to be talking to. I did not have a great track record of praying for people and them being healed. I was usually the one people called when someone wasn't going to survive. I knew that God was a God of miracles, and I had believed He would heal Pastor Danny and Sheriff Ken. Yet each of them crossed over to heaven.

Was helping Allan's family pray for his recovery the right thing to do, especially after the doctors gave him such a grim prognosis?

Or should I help prepare them to let him go?

Just then the image of a man came to me—the friendly, bearded face of Don Piper.

Don and I met at a faith conference in Seattle the summer before. We talked about his book *90 Minutes in Heaven*, and when we said good-bye, we hugged and I kissed his cheek. Here was a man who had been dead for ninety minutes—who had been without oxygen far longer than Allan—and yet I had kissed his face! Run over by a truck, no heartbeat, no breathing, no vital signs, nothing—yet I had stood onstage with him as he shared his story! You couldn't get a worse prognosis than Don's—he was pronounced dead at the scene of the crash and had even been covered up with a tarp—and yet somehow he lived.

And that is what I told Frankye in the waiting room while her own son was down the hall fighting for his life.

Frankye looked at me and said, "I was just saying to God, 'I believe You are a God of miracles, and I want You to show the world there are still miracles today.'"

She was right. There *are* miracles today. Yes, I had prayed over people whom God did not physically heal, but that did not mean God wouldn't choose to heal Allan. God is the One "Who gives life to the dead and calls into being things that were not" (Romans 4:17). And we who believe in that power can speak it into existence through prayer. When we pray and believe, the chance for a miracle is always there. And until God tells us otherwise, we must keep believing in the miracle.

"The doctors may be telling you there is no hope," I said to Frankye, "but Allan is still breathing; his heart is still beating. God is the only true physician, and as we wait for His final answer to come, we will stand in the yes."

This became our mantra as we prayed for Allan—to stand in the yes.

Frankye brought me in to see Allan. He was in a coma and connected to a ventilator. I walked over to the side of his bed and gently placed my hand on top of his.

"Allan, I know what you must be seeing at this very moment," I said. "I know that your angels are with you, and I know how beautiful it all is. But I also know you haven't gone through the gates yet."

My mind raced back to the moments I stood in the presence of God, not far from the entrance to heaven, and God said, "Once we get there, you cannot come back." All I had to do was go through those gates. But I never did.

"Allan, I know your spirit doesn't want to come back, but I believe God has a divine appointment for you here," I said. "You have a world that needs to know about the God you love."

Then I told Frankye, who was a Methodist minister, to keep praying as hard as she could. "Remember that when I died, I could hear my mother while I was in heaven," I said. "I couldn't hear anyone else, but I could hear my mother. And it was her prayers that brought me back."

Frankye wiped the tears from her eyes and hugged me again.

"I will let him go when God gives me peace to do so," she said. "But God hasn't given me peace yet, so I know his story isn't over."

A few days later Kelly called me again. She was talking so fast I had to tell her to slow down.

"Crystal, I had a dream last night," she said, "and I woke up with someone screaming, 'Allan, open your eyes!' And that someone was *me*!"

Kelly later told me how, after the dream, she rushed to the hospital and prayed over Allan. The doctors had told his family that if he didn't start showing improvement by a certain day, it would be time to start thinking about taking him off the ventilator. That day, Kelly told me, was the day after her dream. In the hospital Kelly took Allan's hand in hers and said, "In the name of Jesus Christ, open your eyes!"

"And, Crystal," Kelly told me, "we looked at his face and slowly, slowly, Allan opened his eyes!"

Over the next few days Allan opened his eyes several more times. His breathing improved, and eventually doctors took him off the ventilator. His vital signs were all good, and a neurologist told the family Allan had responded to prompts for the first time. He tried to move his lips to talk and performed small tasks on command.

One day, the lead neurologist examined Allan and gave his family an update.

"I am very pleased," the neurologist said. "It's a miracle."

Today, his family writes on their blog, "Allan continues to make small improvements and we wait expectantly for the full manifestation of God's miracle."

My mother believed in the miracle and prayed me back to earth. Now I was able to watch Frankye do the same with her son, Allan. And Kelly, who knows the pain and grief of losing a son, now comforts Frankye—a mom praying for her own child to make it. Together, I believe, we are all getting to witness another miracle. We come before God and we expect His answer to be yes.

How can I believe in this? Because God gives me confirmations all the time.

Even in the waiting room where we sat with Allan's family.

As we sat and talked there, we learned that when Frankye was a child she went to a little two-room church on a dirt road in the tiny rural town of Gibson Station.

Incredibly, when Virgil's mother, Eddie, was a child, she went to the same tiny church in the same tiny town at the very same time!

"We were all there together for years," Frankye said. "I played the piano for the choir and your aunts and your momma sang in it. Oh my gosh, that must have been over fifty years ago! And now here you are!"

In my mind I could see young Frankye and Eddie laughing and singing in that dusty little church half a century ago. And in the hospital, I could see how God brought their sons together—two strangers who lived hundreds of miles apart—so that one could pray over the other! It was overwhelming!

Some will say it was merely coincidence.

But to me it wasn't a coincidence. It was a confirmation from God.

Why do I pray for the sick and dying to survive while at the same time telling them how amazing and desirable heaven is? Why do I cling so desperately to the living, if letting them go means they'll be in their true and glorious home?

Because the passage to heaven is indescribably wondrous, but for the people left behind, it's filled with heartache and pain.

I can see the irony of someone who's been to heaven praying to keep others out of it, at least for a while longer. But the fact is, no matter how much I can't wait to get back to heaven, it is *not* okay when I lose someone I love. I am comforted by my knowledge of where they've gone, but I still grieve their loss, and I still feel great heartbreak, and I still get mad because I can't call them to share a joke or email them a funny photo. Yes, of course, I *want* them to go to heaven, I *want* them to feel what I felt.

Just not yet.

This is one of the things I've had to grapple with—and still grapple with—since coming back from heaven: Why do I get distraught when people close to me pass? Shouldn't I feel gleeful? Why is it so hard to let them go?

I know it might not make much sense, but I figure it's because I am human. And yes, I'll admit it, I'm selfish. Life is so very precious, and I really like hugging people, and when I can't do that with someone anymore, it hurts.

And so I prayed for Allan to survive, and I cheered when doctors took him off the ventilator, and I praised God for working a miracle. Do the miracles we ask for always come to pass? No. But that doesn't mean we shouldn't expect them to.

I do not know what the journey for Allan is going to look like from here on in. But I strongly hope that one day he will be able to sit up and tell me about his own heaven experience. And I know that in this moment, I believe in the miracle that is coming. Because until God says His answer is no, those of us who love Allan will all continue to stand in the yes.

CHAPTER THIRTEEN

Where Love Lives

THE TOWN WHERE I GREW UP, AND WHERE I STILL live, is right in the middle of Tornado Alley, a huge stretch of the Great Plains where many tornadoes hit. The state directly above us, Kansas, has more tornadoes per square mile than any state in the country, but Oklahoma is a close second. The wail of tornado warning sirens blaring in the air was one of the most common sounds of my childhood—and it still is today.

Not long ago, I was home with Virgil and the twins and my teenage daughter, Sabyre (my son Payne was away), when a warning siren ripped through the air. We knew what to do; we'd rehearsed it often enough. Virgil and I rounded up all of our kids, dogs, and pillows and piled into the bathtub—all within sixty seconds of the siren going off. We stayed huddled in the tub until the siren stopped, but even afterward the twins, then just six years old, were pretty spooked. We let them sleep with us in our bed that night.

For most of my life, I was nearly crippled by my fear of death. I was terrified by all the different ways I could die. I could drown or get hit by a car or be in a fire or, of course, be swept up by one of those tornadoes. But going to heaven changed all that—the experience wiped away *all* my fears of dying. Now, do I like the uncertainty of not knowing when I'm going to die? No. I would love it if God could send me a letter that reads, "Hey, Crystal, I'll meet you next Tuesday for lunch." But am I afraid of dying? Not anymore—not after heaven.

I am, however, still afraid for my kids.

As parents, we do everything in our power to keep our kids safe. That is just a basic human instinct. But ultimately their safety in the world is not something that's within our power to control.

Sometimes we need to rely on God's grace.

Sometimes all we can do is pray the world will be good to our kids.

A few months before I died, I was unloading my car outside my home one fall afternoon when two young men came up from behind me and asked me if I needed help. Without even looking up, I knew who they were—the Mormon missionaries.

I saw them around town all the time. I always tried to smile at them, while also trying to avoid any kind of conversation.

"No thanks," I hollered over my shoulder as I grabbed one of the many grocery bags spilling out of my trunk.

"Okay," one of the young men said. "If you ever need any help, just let us know. We would love to come and talk to you."

"Yeah, okay," I grunted as I continued wrestling with my groceries.

"Maybe tomorrow after lunch?" the other young man asked, reaching over to help me close my trunk.

"Sure," I muttered absently, finally escaping them with my arms straining under the weight of the groceries and my feet kicking a fallen box of cereal toward my front door.

I assumed they understood that when I said, "Sure," I was just being polite.

But then, the next afternoon, I heard a soft knock on the door.

I was right in the middle of a moment I looked forward to every day—the moment when I got my twins down for a nap. Don't get me wrong: I *loved* spending time with my children. But every mommy needs a little time each day to sit in silence and do nothing and just breathe for a few minutes. That's just what I was doing, cozied up on the sofa with a blanket over me and a magazine in my hands. I'd even taped a note above the doorbell asking visitors not to ring or knock loudly, lest they wake my sleeping babies.

Then I heard footsteps outside, followed at first by silence, and then a soft knock.

I looked at a clock—12:45 p.m. I scrunched up my face as I realized who was knocking.

Crud! I thought as I held my breath and froze in place on the sofa. I contemplated the next move and considered all my options. Then I did what any self-respecting mother of four would do during naptime.

I slithered down off the sofa like a snake and lay on the floor so the boys couldn't see me through the glass panel on the front door.

I lay there for several minutes, my face pressed against the carpet, trying to breath as quietly as possible, until I was sure they were gone.

And let me tell ya, I didn't feel bad about doing it, either. I went to church every Sunday and I simply wasn't interested in spending any more time talking about a God Who I wasn't sure was even listening anyway.

But then I died, and I learned God was *always* listening.

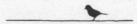

After heaven, my life looked a lot different than it had before. I was now someone who *loved* going into people's homes and talking to them about God's love. I was traveling the country telling people about how God changed my life. I also led Bible studies for women in my home. It was during one of these study sessions that my friend Kelli mentioned the Mormon missionary boys stopping by her house.

"They are just so sweet," she said as we all finished making plates of food in the kitchen. "They always ask if they can do anything to help us. They even offered to come mow our lawn. I would just love to cook them dinner sometime and get to know them better."

Kelli is such a kind and loving person, and she'd spent many afternoons on her front porch talking with the missionaries. She was devout in her own faith and she had no interest in being taught anything different than what she already believed. But she *was* interested in making the boys feel loved and welcomed. She told us how she'd witnessed other neighbors being rude or unwelcoming to the boys, and how much that bothered her.

Of course I thought back to how I had been so dismissive of them earlier in my life. But that had been before God changed me. After heaven, I felt like I loved all people regardless of our differences. It is not a stretch to say that I began to see God in everyone.

Suddenly, I felt a deep longing to let the missionaries know that, although we might not believe the same things, they were welcome in my home anytime.

We all agreed to host a dinner for the boys, and Kelli invited them to my house for Bible study the following week. Our friend Sarah, who was part of our group, would also be there. Sarah had been partly raised Mormon. When her parents divorced, she spent half her time in the Baptist church and the other half in the Mormon church. She told us her older brother had gone on a two-year mission just like the boys we saw bicycling around town. That made me feel even worse about how I'd treated them.

The night of the dinner, right on time, my doorbell rang. Kelli led four young men into the living room. When I saw them I thought, *Wow, they're just kids.* They were wearing their traditional white shirts and black ties, and they just looked so *young.* None of them seemed like they could have been any older than eighteen. The boys were all funny, friendly, cheerful, and outgoing—right away we all clicked. They were excited to see the lasagna and desserts we'd prepared for them, and even more excited when we told them they could take any leftovers home.

One of the boys introduced himself as Elder Bueller. When I was making drinks for the boys, I called out from the kitchen, "Would any of you like more tea? Bueller? Bueller? Bueller?" He laughed as I handed him his tea, and he said people quoted the movie *Ferris Bueller's Day Off* to him all the time.

My son Payne, who was about the same age as the boys, smelled the lasagna and came out of his room. Payne has always had a very strong faith, and throughout the evening I could hear him talking to the boys about their different beliefs. No one had any expectations. No one was interested in denouncing anybody else's faith. It was just an easy sharing of beliefs between people who felt equally sure of their understanding of God, as different as those understandings may have been.

Before he slipped away, Payne invited the boys to come back and watch a movie or TV sometime.

"We're not allowed to watch television," one of the boys answered.

Payne looked absolutely stunned.

"No TV?" he said. "Man, I would hate that."

For the rest of the night we all talked, shared, laughed, and told jokes. At one point, the conversation turned more serious. One of the boys told us about the day he lost his little brother to cancer. His parents had asked the little boy what he wanted for Christmas, which was just weeks away.

"All I want for Christmas are toys for the other kids in the hospital," the little boy answered.

To this day, the young missionary told us, his family hosts an annual toy drive at the hospital in honor of his brother, who passed away at the age of six—not too much older than my own son Micah. Losing his brother was heartbreaking, he told us, but it also helped to shape his faith.

"It helped me turn toward God," he said, "not away from Him."

He also explained that his family's belief in heaven—the understanding they would all be together again someday—brought them great comfort and hope. I told him how sorry I was for the loss of his little brother. I shared with him what I knew to be true about heaven. In that moment, I didn't see our differences. All I saw were people sharing about their lives, their faith, and the moments that had changed them.

After a while, I asked the boys, "Do people treat you well in the towns you visit?"

All four of them got really quiet and looked at each other. Finally, the oldest of the four spoke up.

"For the most part," he said.

"What do you mean?" I asked.

The boys explained how they'd been yelled at by people in passing cars, chased by unleashed dogs, and shooed away by home owners who slammed their doors instead of just closing them. I was horrified, but the boys assured us they were fine. They said they just laughed it off and went on with their business. It was just part of the deal. Besides, they said, the good always outweighed the bad, and all situations were teachable moments.

I was amazed by their wisdom and strength and devotion. They were willing to leave their families and live in distant cities in order to share what they believed with complete strangers. The boys admitted they missed their families deeply, and explained they were allowed to call their mothers only twice a year— Mother's Day and Christmas. Yet none of that deterred them from their mission. When it came to proclaiming their faith, I had to hand it to these boys—they were bold and courageous.

That night, after the boys left, I posted a couple of photos of them on my social media page and described our wonderful dinner together.

"Sometimes," I wrote, "it is nice to simply lay down the denominational lines and just love each other."

Not for a moment did I ever expect what happened next. Within moments comments began to appear.

They were similar to the comments about my appearance on TV—harsh, cruel, and hateful.

"They're in a cult," people wrote of the Mormon boys. "They are brainwashed."

"They don't believe in God."

"They don't believe in Jesus."

"They aren't Christians."

"They're polygamists."

"Shame on you, Crystal."

The negative reaction surprised me, but I can't say I completely blamed these critics. Before I died and went to heaven, I very well may have acted the same way. One of the greatest things I took away from my time in heaven was an awareness of the inconceivable, limitless amount of love that God radiates for us all. The moment I experienced God's love in heaven, I knew it was truly the most powerful thing I'd ever felt—and ever would feel.

Jesus knew that kind of love. He gave that kind of love, and He taught that kind of love. "Love the Lord your God with all your heart and with all your soul and with all your strength and with all your mind," He instructs in Luke 10:27. "Love your neighbor as yourself." How could I love God but not love the very people He created, regardless of our differences? These kind, brave boys, plain and simple, were my neighbors. Jesus didn't say to love our neighbors only if they believe the same things we do. His instruction was to love our neighbors *whoever* they are.

When I think about the neighbors who are intertwined in my life, it is impossible not to see the beauty within each one of them. I have friends who are Christian, Muslim, and Buddhist. Some don't believe in anything at all. I have gay friends and straight friends and friends of every race and nationality. I have friends who are judgmental, friends who are judges. I have friends who are doctors, aid workers, and missionaries, and others who are felons, addicts, and prostitutes. I have friends who serve in our military, friends who are homeless, and friends who are millionaires. The thought of not having a single one of these friends in my life makes me impossibly sad. We may all be very different, but one common factor remains.

We were all created by the very same God.

For that reason, I didn't get mad when I read the nasty comments about the missionaries. Instead, I felt sorry for the people who responded with such hate. And I hoped they might one day know the kind of love and generosity I saw in the faces of those boys.

There was one more online comment that made me take notice.

"Crystal," it read, "one of those boys is my son. Thank you for loving him."

It came from the mother of one of our guests that night. She also contacted me privately and told me her son was allowed to send her only one email a week, and in his one email he told her all about our dinner. She told me how comforting it was for her to know that someone had taken in her son, fed him, talked to him, and loved him for a while. She told me how proud she was of him, but she also confessed how much she missed him and how deeply she worried about him.

"I can't imagine what that must be like," I said.

The love for her son that came through in her message was more powerful than all the hate in the other comments combined.

A couple of days later I showed up to volunteer at the office of the charitable group where I met Sue and Lori. Paula, the director, smiled at me and said, "Crystal, your four friends are here."

I walked in to find the missionaries sitting at a table. During our dinner two days earlier, I'd told them about the work we did, and I'd mentioned we were always looking for volunteers. Still, I hadn't expected to see them there. I'd told lots of people about the group and how badly we needed volunteers, but few people actually came by to help. There were many times when I was too busy to volunteer myself, so I never got upset when people were unable to help. Yet there they were, all four of the boys, happy and eager to pitch in. They spent the morning moving donated furniture, cleaning out the back rooms, and helping stock food.

"They just dove in and started working," Paula said. "They're incredible."

The boys came back each day we were open. Eventually, the time came for them to move on to another town, and I was sad to see them go. But the very next week, I showed up to volunteer and saw four new missionaries waiting outside the front door.

"We were told we could help here," one of them said.

We welcomed them with open arms.

Paula understood that their beliefs differed from the beliefs of some of the founders of the group, so she tended to have them work behind the scenes rather than up front in the office. But when I learned one of the new boys was fluent in Spanish, I often pulled him up front to help me translate for the Spanish-speaking families. The boys were just so giving, charitable, and fun to be around—before long everyone loved them. They became especially close with Paula, and joined her and her family at church on Sundays and on a basketball court Saturday mornings for a pickup game. The special relationship they formed endured even after these boys left, spilling over onto the next rotation of missionaries, and the one after that.

Then one day I showed up early to volunteer and found Paula in her office with her head in her hands. I sat in the chair in front of her desk and asked her what was wrong.

Paula told me that not everyone in town supported the idea of the Mormon boys volunteering there. Some people just didn't feel it was right. Paula told me how she literally had to beg the churches in town for volunteers—and how few people consistently volunteered. Very gently and lovingly, which is true to Paula's character, she also said that—despite how much she loved her job, despite the countless hours of sweat and tears and prayers she poured into it—if the Mormon boys were forced to leave, she would be leaving with them.

"I don't see denominations here," Paula said. "I see people that God desperately loves. And because He first loved us, together we are able to love others."

Paula took a stand. She stood by what she believed. And the Mormon boys got to stay.

Meeting the boys taught me a valuable lesson about what it means to truly love your neighbor, as the Lord taught. Their passion truly inspired me, and after I got to know them I prayed for God to invest me with such passion—to give me the strength to leave my comfort zone and be more missionary for Him. And God didn't take long to answer that prayer, only He didn't answer it in a way I expected.

God did not call me for a mission.

Instead, He called my son.

CHAPTER FOURTEEN

The Third Ward

I WAS ONLY SEVENTEEN YEARS OLD WHEN I LAID MY hand on my stomach and felt the tiny being growing inside me kick for the first time. A powerful wave of love washed over me. It was a love I'd never felt before—deep, unconditional, and everlasting. I hadn't known the human heart could love another person as much as I loved my precious baby boy.

I was experiencing the depths of a mother's love for the first time.

To be completely honest, the idea of having a child scared me. In so many ways, I was still a child myself. When I went to the hospital with contractions, the pain shooting through my body filled me with panic. As soon as one really bad contraction stopped, I flung my feet over the side of the bed and started getting dressed so I could leave.

"Where are you going?" Connie, my mom's best friend and my Lamaze coach, asked me.

"I can't do this; I'm leaving," I replied.

Connie laughed and said, "Honey, it doesn't matter where you go, you're gonna have this baby today."

Even toward the end of my labor, when the nurses cheered me on and assured me the baby was almost here, my only thought was, *Will I ever be able to give this child what he needs?*

But then it happened—I heard the first cry of my sweet little son. In that instant I knew I'd met the love of my life. I named him Jameson Payne.

Together, Payne and I have weathered some really tough storms. The motorcycle crash when he was six years old left him with a broken arm, a mangled leg, and a complete loss of hearing in his right ear. Worst of all, Payne suffered a traumatic brain injury that would soon change all of my family's lives.

After the accident, Payne began exhibiting severe mood swings and terrible outbursts. Often he was so out of control, Virgil or I would wind up intertwined with him on the floor, our arms wrapped around him trying to restrain him. His teachers had a difficult time handling him in school, and therapy didn't seem to help. I spent the first two years after his accident going to hundreds of doctor appointments, begging for answers. After Payne spent five months at an inpatient hospital, we finally began to gather the tools we needed to deal with his injuries.

In spite of all the difficulties, Payne grew up to be a sweet, kind, and loving child. Even as a little boy, he developed a deep inner strength that was remarkable and unique for a child so young. He was passionate and extremely energetic, which left me searching for avenues for all that energy. We tried different sports, but Payne finally found his niche with music.

Then came his teenage years.

As a teen, Payne was incredibly rebellious. After all, he is his

mother's son. He was always exploring, pushing boundaries, acting out. He challenged Virgil and me at every turn, and it felt as
if we were constantly fighting with him about something. There
were lots of door slamming and disrespectful defiance. Even in
the car on the way to church on Sunday mornings, Payne would
argue with us, and we would argue back, until finally I'd have
enough. I'd yell: *"We are going to church and we will worship the
Lord together, and we will be a happy family!"*

And as I stepped out of the van I would smile and wave good
morning to our fellow church members, while at the same time
pulling Payne close and telling him, "Or so help *you*, God."

Someone once said the person who wrote the song with the
lyrics "easy like Sunday morning" never had to get their family
ready for church on time.

As he grew up, Payne began to experience bouts of restlessness
and depression. He was often closed off from the rest of the family
for days at a time. One night, when he was in high school, Payne
told us he was tired of living and planned on taking his own life.

With two teenage suicides in our town that year alone, I
couldn't take his words as just an idle threat. Virgil and I made
some phone calls and decided our best option was to seek more
in-depth professional help. It was not what any of us wanted for
Payne, and when we talked to him about it, he screamed and told
us how much he hated us. Then Payne ran away.

He was picked up by the police later that evening. At the station I watched with a breaking heart as officers handcuffed my
son, put him in the back of their police car, and took him to a psy-
chiatric facility for observation. He was seventeen years old—the
same age I'd been when I kissed his newborn face and promised
to always protect him.

I felt as if I was failing to keep that promise.

Virgil and I drove through the darkness of the night, following Payne in the police car. I thought back to my time in heaven, and I remembered God showing me His perfect plan for my children. But that plan didn't seem so perfect at that moment.

"God," I said to Him, "all his life the enemy has been trying to destroy my son."

And very gently God replied, "That's why I sent Mine."

Payne fought through his struggles and eventually came back home, and the following year I watched him walk across a stage and graduate high school. Virgil and I helped him enroll in the local college, where he planned to pursue a degree in criminal justice. But then, during that first summer after high school, Payne began to challenge us yet again. He began to miss his curfew and was especially disrespectful to Virgil. After several missed curfews—and several punishments that didn't seem to faze him—Virgil sat Payne down for a warning.

"I love you, but I am not running a hotel," Virgil calmly explained. "I don't care if you are nineteen or ninety-nine years old, this is my house. If you miss curfew again, you will no longer be a resident of this home."

A few nights later Payne came home hours past his curfew. Virgil and I were waiting for him in the living room.

"Hey, what's up?" Payne said casually.

"Son, you know I love you," Virgil said.

"Yeah, I love you, too," Payne said.

"I am going to miss you."

Payne was startled. Slowly, he realized what was happening.

"You're kicking me out?" he yelled. "Seriously, you're kicking me out? Who kicks their son out in the middle of the night with nowhere to go?"

I was already sobbing and maybe even faltering in the decision, but Virgil held firm.

"You have ten minutes," he told Payne. "Anything you can't take tonight, we will make arrangements for you to come back for later."

Payne told Virgil that he hated him and didn't want to live with us anyway. He threw some of his clothes in a bag and slammed the front door as hard as he could on his way out. As he did, one of my favorite crosses fell off the wall and shattered against the floor. I knelt down to pick up the pieces, but instead slumped against the wall and broke down in despair. I don't think I've ever felt that helpless.

In the end, that night was the beginning of a turning point for Payne. With nowhere to go, he slept in his car in the church parking lot. When the sun rose, he made his way to his youth leader Henry's house. Henry was a gentle guide, and he spoke the truth of God's Word to Payne that entire weekend. The next week, Payne moved into a small apartment with a friend.

Payne still wasn't ready to patch things up with us, and almost every time we tried to visit him, he sent us away. Not knowing how he was doing or what he was feeling was so incredibly hard for me. All I could do was pray for his safety and try not to worry so much. *Payne will be fine*, I kept telling myself. *Payne will be all right*.

Sadly, he wasn't all right.

On his own for the first time, Payne got lost. He began drinking and smoking and hosting late-night parties. During that time, I prayed *so, so* hard over my son. I just wanted so much more for him than what he seemed to be giving himself. The rare times when he'd come by our house, I was always sure to pull him in for a long hug and tell him how much I loved him. But then he'd disappear and we wouldn't see him or hear from him for several more days. I had a strong suspicion he wasn't doing well, but I had no idea how to help him or get through to him. All I could do was pray, and pray hard.

Then one day my cell rang. It was Payne.

"Mom," he said, "I need to come talk to you and Dad. It's serious."

I paced back and forth in our living room waiting for him to arrive.

"I'm too young to be a grandmother," I told Virgil. "Or do you think he's on drugs? Do you think he's in legal trouble?"

"Crystal, let's just wait and see what he has to tell us," Virgil said.

Not much later, Payne arrived at our home with Henry. We all sat in the living room, and I balled my hands into fists and tried to keep it together. I had no idea what Payne was about to say. Finally, he took a deep breath and spoke.

"I have turned so far away from the Lord," he said, his eyes reddening.

Over the next hour he shared the hurts and pains of his life. The abandonment he felt from his biological father, the anger and frustration he still dealt with from the accident. He told us about the parties and the drinking and how he had spiraled out of control. He also shared his longing for God to help him.

Then Payne told us about the Devil's Armchair.

After he'd been in his new apartment for about three weeks, Payne answered a knock on the front door. It was Henry, reminding him that earlier that year he'd signed up for the church's youth program, and the following week he was supposed to travel with the group to climb a mountain in Colorado. At first, Payne didn't want to go, but Henry convinced him he should.

Their destination was Mount Ouray, a fourteen-thousand-foot peak in the southern part of the Rocky Mountains. The plan was for Payne and the other kids in the youth program to scale the eastern face of the mountain, which is known as the Devil's Armchair. On his first day, after a few hours of lugging his thirty-pound backpack up the first part of the mountain, Payne believed he'd never make it to the top. He was out of shape and he'd started smoking, so the higher he climbed, the more his lungs hurt. On his third day climbing, he got a bad case of elevation sickness. Now he was absolutely certain he'd never make it to camp.

And yet, with the help of his fellow climbers—who graciously divided up the contents of his backpack and carried them for him—Payne made it to the top.

The experience, he told us, changed his life.

"It was the hardest thing I've ever done in my life," he said. "On my way up the mountain I prayed a lot. I knew I wasn't in the place I needed to be and I started to take a good look at myself. I prayed to God about my future and my life."

A week later, Payne told us he had another important announcement he needed to share.

"I am not going to college," he said. "I truly feel God is calling me into missions. I don't know where or how or when, but I do know that I told him yes."

Honestly, I didn't know how to react. I'd spent so much time trying to help Payne get into college, and I'd been on top of all those details, and now he was tossing it all out the window. So instead of congratulating Payne on his brave decision, I think I said something like, "Well, you and God are going to have figure out all the details on that because I'm finished."

Yes, I was grateful Payne had realized how lost he was, and I was happy he was so devoted to finding his way back to God. But I wasn't sure this was the way to go. The only thing I could do was pray and let God do His work. I told Payne that if God truly was calling him on this path, then He would line the path for Payne to walk on.

Within a week Payne had been accepted onto the 2015 mission team with an organization called Mission Year. Mission Year is a yearlong urban ministry program focused on Christian service and discipleship. The tagline on their website says, "One Year Can Change Everything." We would all soon see how right that was.

Payne was assigned to the Third Ward in Houston, Texas. When we told Virgil's father, who was from the Houston area, he warned us about the neighborhood.

The more I researched it, the further my heart sank.

The Third Ward is one of six historic wards in Houston, and it's just southeast of the downtown area. The singer Beyoncé was born and raised there. Today, it is like many underprivileged urban areas in the United States—it has problems with drugs and crime.

In fact, a 2013 crime study listed the Third Ward as the fifteenth most dangerous neighborhood in America.

My son was headed there for a year.

All my protective instincts kicked in, and I spent the next few weeks worried to death about Payne's safety. I had prayed to God to watch over my son. I had asked God to pluck him out of the wilderness and put him on the right path. But I hadn't known God was going to pluck him out of his wilderness and drop him into the Third Ward! I shared some of my concerns with Payne, but his mind was already made up. He was leaving and there was nothing we could do to stop him.

The day arrived for us to say our good-byes. We helped him pack up all his belongings from his apartment and get them into storage, and we woke up early to drive him to the airport to catch his early morning flight. The twins snuggled with Payne in the backseat, enjoying their last moments with him for a while. I sat quietly in the front seat, not at all sure of what I was feeling. I was afraid that if I said even one word, the floodgate of tears would open.

We walked with Payne until we couldn't continue through the security checkpoint. I watched as he hugged his sisters, his brother, and Virgil. Then it was my turn.

"Mom, I'm going to be fine," Payne told me. He may have looked like a man as he towered over me, but in my eyes and in my heart he was forever my baby boy. Payne wrapped his arms around me and finally I started to cry. I wiped my eyes and pulled one of my favorite books out of my bag.

It was called *The Irresistible Revolution* by Shane Claiborne.

Shane is a young social activist and strong Christian warrior who has put his faith into practice in a way very few people have. He has worked with Mother Teresa in Calcutta and ministered to the needy in war-torn Baghdad. He has sacrificed and taken risks in order to do God's work in some of the darkest places on earth. His ideas about what it means to live a truly Christian lifestyle—and to be what he calls "an ordinary radical"—are very moving to me.

I handed Payne the book. Then I hugged him one last time and gave him a kiss good-bye. I knew that when he sat down in the plane and opened the book, he would see, on one of the first pages, the simple message I wrote to him:

Welcome to the Revolution.

I had believed God would choose me for a mission. But as the book passed from my hand into Payne's, I realized God had chosen him all along.

Payne called once he got settled in Houston and let us know he was living in a house with several other friendly kids his age. "I'm okay," he assured me. "This is going to be great." I could hear the excitement in his voice, and some of the gut-level fear went away. Some of it, but not all of it. A year is a long time.

It would be a few more months before I got the terrifying call that filled me with dread and panic.

My son had been attacked and beaten.

CHAPTER FIFTEEN

Star of Hope

I
T WAS PAYNE HIMSELF WHO CALLED TO TELL ME
what happened.

"Momma," he said at the start of the call, "I just want you to
know I'm okay."

Which struck me as code for "Something had happened."

"What do you mean, you're okay?" I asked, my voice rising.

"I got jumped and beat up," Payne said.

I gasped and nearly dropped the phone. Payne went into
more detail about the attack, but it was hard to pay attention. I
was too emotional. I heard something about how he was knocked
to the ground and kicked, and how his attackers laughed as they
beat him. All I could do was keep saying the same two words over
and over again.

"Come home," I said. "Come home."

"Mom," Payne said, "I can't come home."

"Why not?!"

"Because," Payne said, "this is exactly why I'm here. Those guys who attacked me have to live in this environment their whole lives. I have to stay here for *them*."

Hearing that your child was hurt is a nightmare for any parent. I felt so much pain and fear and anger. I was mad. In fact, I was furious. My first thought was, *How dare anyone rob and beat my son? How dare anyone hurt him?* The thought of Payne lying on the ground, all alone, being kicked and beaten as his attackers laughed, made me cry so hard I threw up.

"This isn't fair," I yelled out to God after the phone call. "I'm so angry!"

"Give it to Me," God responded.

"I'm so afraid for my son!"

"Give him to Me," God said.

The truth is, I had already surrendered Payne to God the day I put him on that plane. I knew I couldn't be there to help him make decisions or try to guide him in the right direction. We got to talk on the phone only once or twice a week, so for the most part I didn't really know what Payne's day-to-day life was like. I didn't know, for instance, if he was okay with being in the Third Ward, or if, like me, he woke up every day terrified. Not knowing if he was struggling or in danger was excruciating. All I could do was ask God to keep watching over my boy.

It was only much later, when Payne wrote about his mission year, that I got the chance to understand what he went through. I want to share some of his writings with you, to give you a feel of what his life was like in the Third Ward.

From Payne:

When I heard I would be going to the Third Ward and learned how dangerous people said it was, I was nervous. You don't just go to a place like that and not get nervous. But it didn't shake my resolve one bit. My mom kind of freaked out about it, and she kept asking me if I was sure this was what I wanted to do. I told her I was sure. It's not like she was trying to talk me out of going or anything like that, it's just that she was worried about my safety. She wanted me to be prepared for what I might find.

Me and seven other volunteers stayed in a two-story house on Beulah Street. Inside there was a living room, a small kitchen, and another unfinished room under the stairs where we kept our bikes. The bedrooms were upstairs, and my roommate Brent and I had two twin-size mattresses on the floor. One of the first things we did was take a tour of the neighborhood. Our city directors wanted us to learn about our surroundings. My first impression was that there was a lot of trash. Trash everywhere. Broken TVs, burned-out furniture, construction debris, garbage bags—all out on the street, out in the open.

On Mondays through Thursdays, I went to work at the biggest homeless shelter in Houston, the Star of Hope Women & Family Emergency Shelter. From eight thirty in the morning to four thirty in the afternoon, I did a lot of different things there. I guess you could say I was like guest services. I cleaned up and helped the residents and did whatever needed to be done.

One day, an ambulance pulled up and dropped off a middle-aged woman. I came to know her as Miss W. Like a lot of people at the shelter, Miss W. had some kind of mental illness. Someone told me she was a paranoid schizophrenic. When she arrived, she was wearing a thin paper hospital gown and nothing else. No dress, no shoes, nothing. She sat in the reception area talking to herself. After a while she threw up all over her hospital gown. I felt sorry for her, and secretly felt really bad for whoever had to clean her up. Then the shelter manager came over and handed me a pair of latex gloves and a roll of paper towels.

I went over and said hello to Miss W. She looked up at me and said something I couldn't hear. I told her I was going to help clean her up. That seemed to make her happy. She was very loving, but she was not in the same place as me. Her mind seemed detached in that moment. I went ahead and did the best I could to help her.

Over the next three days, the people who were supposed to come and assist her—the therapists, counselors, and health care workers—never showed up. So I stayed with her, talking and trying to entertain her. She said she liked to draw, so we drew pictures together. She asked me to read the Bible to her, and I read her Genesis. One day she pulled me close and whispered something to me.

"You know what you are?" she said. "You are an angel from heaven."

She talked about my wings and how pure the light was around me. I was a bit freaked out. I had that image in my mind all day. That night, back at home, I cried. Why? Because this woman who was suffering from mental illness saw me more clearly than I could have ever seen myself. She looked at me and knew that all my sins didn't matter.

"I have no family," she told me one day while we sat together and did our drawings, "but that's okay because I have you, my angel."

Finally, two health care workers arrived to take Miss W. away. I was upset to see that they were kind of rude and dismissive toward her. They didn't bother to help her down the ramp in front of the shelter, so I walked her to the car. The health care workers were laughing and paying her no mind as she struggled to get into the car. Just before she got in, I asked if I could pray with her. We said a quick prayer and then we hugged. I gave her a picture I had drawn for her—a picture of a great big, green tree.

"You're going to be okay," I said.

She nodded.

I helped Miss W. into the backseat, closed the door, and watched the car drive away. I have never felt so helpless in my life. It is one thing to feel helpless for yourself, but another thing entirely to feel helpless for someone else.

In my time at the shelter, I met a lot of people who were broken down. Beaten down physically, mentally, and spiritually. They were living lives that were just impossibly hard. What we tried to do at the shelter was give them at least a few of the tools they needed to get back on their feet. We offered people a room to stay in. We gave them supplies like shampoo, toothpaste, toilet paper, baby wipes, and diapers. We connected people with caseworkers who helped prepare them for job interviews.

Seeing all these people really hurt my heart, but it also changed the way I looked at them—and at myself. All along I'd been thinking of myself as a missionary. But that's not what I was at all.

No—I was a neighbor.

Eventually I stopped thinking of the Third Ward as a dangerous place, and I began thinking of it as a community. A community I was part of. And the people I was meeting weren't charity cases or lost souls—they were my friends.

About a week before Thanksgiving, I had a one-on-one meeting with my Mission Year director. We met in a coffee shop not far from the shelter. We talked for about an hour, and then, around 6:30 p.m., I got on my bicycle and started riding the two miles back to my house on Beulah Street. The bike path ran across a highway and through a pretty rough neighborhood. We weren't supposed to go out on our own at night, but that evening was unusual because of my meeting. I started pedaling down the bike path and got nearly all the way to McGowen Street, about ten blocks from where I lived.

Then, up ahead, I saw a group of teenagers, six in all, walking on the bike path. They were blocking my way, and I thought about turning around, but where was I going to go? I had already passed the road and had two ditches on either side of me. All I could do was slow down and bike toward the group. At the last second they parted and let me pass.

I'm okay, I thought. *Nothing to worry about.*

But before I made it all the way by them, I saw something out of the corner of my left eye. It was a hand balled into a fist. The fist hit me in the face, hard. Somehow I stayed on my bike, and I started pedaling faster, but the grass slowed me down. I felt someone punch me in the face again. I fell off the bike and landed in the grass alongside the bike path. I was ready to use all the boxing moves my dad taught me, but two or three of the teenagers jumped on top of me, while the others punched and kicked me from above. One of them kicked me hard in the face.

My first instinct was to get up, defend myself, and fight them off. I was ready to go down fighting. But then, suddenly, I felt nothing but calm. I felt a presence inside me that told me to be still. I made the choice to act like they had knocked me out. It was the hardest choice I have ever made. I lay on the ground protecting my face with my limp hand as I let them punch and kick me. After a while I heard them start to laugh and brag about how they'd knocked me out. One of them took my backpack and ripped it open. All I had inside were Christian books I was reading for curriculum and some poems I had been writing. The teenager poured the books out on top of me.

They stole my wallet, my bicycle, and my helmet, kicking me a couple more times before running off. I stayed on the ground for a few more seconds, then got to my feet. What hurt the most was that they had taken my wallet. I didn't have any money in it, but I did have a small photo of my younger sister Willow and my brother Micah. Losing that photo made me angrier than I could have imagined.

I checked myself to see what damage had been done. I was pretty sure I had a black eye, but remarkably I wasn't bleeding. I had a ton of bruises and my ribs were sore, but luckily I'd been wearing a heavy leather jacket, and though they hit me pretty hard, they didn't hurt me too bad. Pretty quickly I realized that things could have turned out much, much worse. All in all, I got off easy.

God, I realized, had His hands all over the situation. God protected me.

I walked the rest of the way home, afraid I might run into the gang again. When I got to Beulah Street I told one of our neighbors, Mr. James, that I'd been jumped. Mr. James is over fifty, but he became so angry that he got into his van and drove around trying to find the teenagers who mugged me. I guess I was glad he didn't find them, but even more so, I was moved by how protective he was of me. Mr. James was one of the best neighbors I've ever had. He treats his neighbors like they are family. By the end of our time together, I felt like we really were family.

Police officers showed up after forty-five minutes and wrote up the incident as a robbery. Not even assault. One of them looked at me sympathetically and said, "This happens all the time." That night, I went to bed feeling angry. I mean, really angry. I wanted to track down the guys who jumped me and get revenge. I had a hard time falling asleep, but when I woke up the next morning all those hostile feelings were gone. It was as if God had visited me in the night and taken them. I lost all my anger and hatred for them. Not because of any choice I'd made, but because God had other plans.

That day, the Mission Year directors sat down with me and helped me come to terms with what had happened. Their love and concern was overwhelming. By the end of the day, all I felt for the men who attacked me was love. I understood there was so much hurt in the Third Ward, and that was exactly the reason why I'd been sent there. I hadn't been sent there to get angry or to hate. I'd been sent there to love. I sat down and I prayed for those men, and I asked God to help them get through their difficult lives. Whatever it was that drove them to do what they did, I prayed God might help them overcome it. I prayed He would force them into submission for Him, like He had done with me.

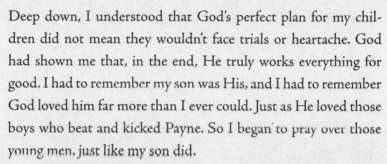

Deep down, I understood that God's perfect plan for my children did not mean they wouldn't face trials or heartache. God had shown me that, in the end, He truly works everything for good. I had to remember my son was His, and I had to remember God loved him far more than I ever could. Just as He loved those boys who beat and kicked Payne. So I began to pray over those young men, just like my son did.

Praying for people I cared about was easy, but it was an entirely different thing to pray for someone who had hurt my child. Yet that is exactly what God led me to do. And it was through that prayer that God removed my fear and anger. The Lord taught us to pray for those who have trespassed against us, and so I did.

But even so, I couldn't help but ask myself, was helping someone to know God's love worth my own son's life?

I was aware that there were Christian missionaries being killed in countries all around the world. I knew that going into the dark corners of the world to bring the message of the Lord and His unfailing love came with some very real risks. Most of all, I knew that even though I trusted in God to protect Payne, that did not mean no harm would come to him. That was not an easy truth for me to accept.

"Is it worth it?" I asked. "Would it be worth my own son's life? Do I truly love God enough to believe my son's life is worth offering to Him?"

The flesh part of me said no. Even though I had been to heaven, and even though I understood God's plan for us is not always ours to know, I still went back and forth with God about many things. I still brought Him my questions, my struggles, and my emotions. No matter what happened to me in heaven, I am still human. We all are. For me, being a Christian doesn't mean I am anywhere near perfect. It simply means I follow the One Who is.

But while the flesh part of me said no, my spirit, the part that had been with God, knew that if Payne was able to show even one person the redemption and salvation of Christ, it would have all been worth it.

And in the end, God did what I, Payne's mother, had never been able to do.

He saved my son.

Even in the phone call when Payne told me he'd been attacked, I sensed a kind of calm in his voice that I'd never really heard before. He just kept assuring me that he was all right, that the Mission Year directors and his fellow missionaries were taking care of him, and that even the neighbors who had become his friends were watching over him. Without trying to, Payne was convincing me that he wasn't the same Payne who missed curfews and fought with his parents all the time. His experience in the Third Ward was fundamentally changing who he was.

This is how Payne himself put it in his writings:

Before I got to Houston, I didn't believe in many things. I had a lot of opinions, but I didn't have any real, deep beliefs. I knew that Jesus was my Lord and Savior and I had the basics down pretty well. I thought I was a good and loving person, but really, I wasn't. I didn't really understand what that meant.

But now I do. The Bible says to love our neighbors as ourselves. But it took Miss W., Mr. James, and so many other good people I met in the Third Ward to teach me what it *means* to love your neighbor.

It means to love people for no other reason than that they're God's children.

I stayed in the Third Ward for a full year, and when it was time to leave I was sorry to go. I felt sad knowing that this chapter of my life was coming to a close. It was difficult to imagine being in any other environment. Back home, I got accepted at the University of Central Oklahoma, where I plan to study forensic science and criminal justice. One day I hope to become a forensic scientist. I think my time in the Third Ward will greatly help me in that line of work. For one thing, I will never again look at people in underprivileged neighborhoods the same way. They may be different from me, but they are not less than me. We are all children of God.

What kind of person will I grow to finally be? I can't say for sure, but I hope that I will be someone who makes his whole life a mission. Someone who got tired of just sitting in a church pew. Someone who takes action. Someone who continues to love all people. A man who knows that sometimes you just have to shut up and listen to God tell you what He wants you to do.

Mission Year has a motto: "Love God, love people."

That is all we have to do.

The Bible came to life for me in the Third Ward. And now this is how I plan to live the rest of my life—as a man on a mission for God. A man who will always love God and love people.

Payne's experience made me think back to the Mormon boys. Like him, they were determined to put their faith into practice. They made sacrifices and stepped into an often hostile world for their faith. When we had the boys over for dinner, I had no idea that just a few months later it would be my own son who would be welcomed into the homes of strangers and forever changed because of their kindness.

I got to meet one of those "strangers" when Virgil and I visited Payne in Houston. Her name was Miss Andre, and she was Payne's coworker at Star of Hope. Miss Andre was the one who took my son close to her—teaching, mentoring, and loving him. When I got to meet her, I gave her a big hug and thanked her for loving my son so deeply while he was there.

One night near the end of Payne's mission year, I overheard Virgil talking to him on speakerphone. I heard Payne apologize to Virgil for being disrespectful, and I heard him say how much he appreciated him.

"You have taught me more about being a man than you will ever know," Payne said. "You taught me how to love God and my family. You never gave up on me, even when I gave up on myself. You never once made me feel as if I was just a stepson."

"That's because you're not," Virgil said. "You are my son."

"Love is patient, love is kind," it says in 1 Corinthians 13:4–8. "It does not envy, it does not boast, it is not proud. It does not dishonor others, it is not self-seeking, it is not easily angered, it keeps no record of wrongs. Love does not delight in evil but rejoices with the truth. It always protects, always trusts, always hopes, always perseveres."

Love is truly the only weapon strong enough to change the world. I have heard my son say, "I went on a mission because I wanted to change people's lives, but they ended up changing mine."

That, right there, is the power of God's love.

CHAPTER SIXTEEN

Love First,
Ask Questions Later

E VERY SINGLE ONE OF US HAS SOMETHING THAT
God placed deep inside us. It is the thing God uses to spread
His love through us. It may be a talent, a skill, an instinct, or a
calling—it is different for each of us. But we all have it deep in our
hearts—as part of our identities as children of God.

But here's the thing—having it is very different from *acting*
on it.

"As the Father has sent me," Jesus says in John 20:21, "I am
sending you." I believe we are not meant to love God in tidy
seclusion—we are meant to take God's love out into the world.
It's a pretty fantastic idea if you think about it. *We are the
agents through which God's love is shared and made real.* "There-
fore go and makes disciples of all nations, baptizing them in
the name of the Father and of the Son and of the Holy Spirit"
(Matthew 28:19).

Some people refer to this obligation to act as the Great Commission.

My friend Jeremy Courtney simply calls it "preemptive love."

In 2006 Jeremy, his wife, Jessica, and their one-year-old daughter, Emma, moved from their home in the United States all the way to Iraq, which was in the middle of a devastating war. There he cofounded the Preemptive Love Coalition, an international organization that provides lifesaving heart surgeries to Iraqi children and training for local doctors and nurses. Since he moved his family to what might be the most dangerous place on earth, Jeremy and his organization have helped arrange more than one thousand heart surgeries for Iraqi children and provided emergency aid to more than seven thousand people.

The story of Jeremy's remarkable sacrifice is told in his beautiful book *Preemptive Love,* in which he shares his simple motto:

Love first, ask questions later.

So what exactly is preemptive love? "Preemptive love actually seeks out the hurting, broken, and unlovely and jumps into the mess of life to join God in 'making all things new,'" Jeremy explains. "It doesn't mean we love ignorantly or blindly . . . it's about loving past all the acceptable reasons for withholding love."

Here was someone who moved his family into the middle of a *war* in order to spread God's love! Talk about getting out of your comfort zone. I marveled at his courage, and I admired that he didn't stand on either side of the religious divide in Iraq. He loves Muslim children just as much as he loves Christian children. To Jeremy, there is no "them." There is only "us."

Even so, those divisions exist, in spite of his love. Recently, soldiers from ISIS went into the Iraqi city of Mosul and marked the doors for Christian families with the red letter *N* for Nazarene, or Christian. These families faced execution if they didn't pay a hefty fine or convert to Islam, and most of them fled the city and took refuge in the mountains. There they confronted a terrible choice—stay on the mountain and face dying of the elements, or go back to the city and likely be killed by ISIS troops. At least forty thousand Iraqis were trapped on what one person called "the mountain from hell."

Jeremy and his family stayed. They sought refuge in God in prayer and worship, and they refused to stop loving.

Jeremy's devotion and love for God demonstrated one of the truest forms of Christianity I'd ever witnessed. It was exactly what my heart had so desperately longed for since I came back from heaven. *This is how we can show the world the love of God*, I thought—*by loving first and asking questions later*.

That's how we can experience heaven on earth. Not by avoiding danger, but by loving in spite of the cost.

When I was in heaven, I crumpled before God and asked Him, "Why didn't I do more for You?" And in the five years since I came back, I have learned there are millions of ways we can all "do more" for God. Some of these ways are gigantic and dramatic—like moving to a war-torn country to spread God's love. But other ways are smaller and simpler—like writing a note of love and compassion and slipping it into a gift bag for a homeless person.

It is important we remember that *all* of the actions in this wide spectrum of "doing more" are beautiful, meaningful, and impactful. The big ones and the little ones—*all* of them are ways God uses us to spread His love. Yes, sometimes God's calling sends people to battlefields halfway around the world. Sometimes God calls us into battles right where we are.

Like the night I joined my friend Michelle W. in a fierce battle with lice.

Michelle is one of the kindest people I know. After years of fertility drugs and endless prayers, she was left wondering if her desire to be a mother would ever be fulfilled. One night, as she watched TV, she saw a commercial depicting the dire need for foster parents. "If I can't have my own children to love," she told God that night, "then I will love whatever children You send me."

Twenty years and more than fifty foster kids later, Michelle called me in tears. Five foster children, all under the age of seven, had just been brought to her home. They were siblings, and they clung to each other with fear in their eyes. Michelle took them in and put what few belongings they had in the bedroom, then knelt down beside them to gently try and ease their fears. When she got close enough, she saw they were all infested with lice.

Out of desperation, and in the fifth hour of battling lice, she called me for help.

It's funny she would think to call me of all people. Not because I wouldn't jump to help her whenever she called, but because Michelle knows that lice just so happen to be one of my biggest phobias.

As a child, I got lice from someone at school and my mom flipped out of her mind. I remember her crying for days as we washed every article of clothing and bedding in the house. I remember I cried when she threw away most of my stuffed animals. It was a three-day ordeal of shampooing, picking, crying, and hurting—not to mention the terror of knowing tiny bugs were crawling all over my head. I began to contemplate what I would look like bald.

The whole experience left me traumatized. Even so, when Michelle called, I pulled my hair back, put on a hat, and went over to help. I called up three other friends and they showed up, too, and we spent the night shampooing the children's hair and picking out bugs. I spent most of my time making the kids laugh so they wouldn't see the panic on my face as I combed through their hair. My friends spent most of their time watching me squirm and laughing.

I noticed that the oldest girl had shoes that didn't fit her feet. I sent out a message online to my friends, who sent it out to their friends. Over the next few hours, people from all over our little town began showing up with brand-new jammies, toiletries, and presents for the children. To see how quickly everyone jumped to help these kids was a really beautiful thing.

Love first, ask questions later.

Introducing people to Christ happens through love, not condemnation or accusations or judgment. Salvation for all of us comes through grace. My time in heaven taught me that God's love is not a passive, theoretical thing. God's love is tangible. We feel it when we put the needs of others before our own, when we tuck our babies into bed—even when we help pick lice out of the hair of sweet children huddled together in a friend's living room. God's love happens all around us, to us, and through us.

God's love is an *action*.

And today, my time on earth is teaching me all the remarkable ways through which we can share that love with others.

A world that desperately needs us to *love first*.

CHAPTER SEVENTEEN

Whispers to the Heart

SOME PEOPLE SAY DREAMS ARE A SUCCESSION OF images, ideas, emotions, and sensations that occur—usually involuntarily—in the mind during sleep.

But to me, dreams are often beautiful connections between God and me.

About two years after I went to heaven, I was startled awake by a dream and sat straight up in bed. Actually, it wasn't much of a dream. In fact, I don't remember what it was about the dream that woke me up with such a start in the early morning hours. I don't remember God saying anything to me. But when I woke up, I felt an intense longing that God had clearly placed within me. A very specific longing that involved two groups of people: those in the homeless community, and my sisters in the adult entertainment industry.

I understood this longing from the start. God wanted me to focus on these two groups. I knew it was a directive from God because I would never have dreamed up such a mission for my self. I wouldn't have dared step that far out of my comfort zone.

Yet as sure as I was that the dream was a communication from God, I wasn't at all sure what He wanted me to do with it. For one thing, I didn't remember seeing any homeless people in my town, and there weren't any strip clubs, either. What on earth was I supposed to do with this new love that had suddenly engulfed my heart?

For the next year or so I couldn't answer that question, so I didn't act on the dream. But I never forgot it, either. I filed it away, and I prayed that one day I would understand what it all meant.

And one day I did.

One of the questions I get asked most frequently is, "How can I talk to God?"

Some people think that because I went to heaven, I have an inside track or a special direct line to God. Often, someone will ask me to pray for something because they imagine God listens to me more than He listens to them. I get a pretty good laugh out of that. I do pray a lot, and all my prayers are answered, but sometimes the answer is no. In fact, God tells me no much more often than He tells me yes.

So, I'm happy to pray for people, but no, I don't have a special pipeline to God. I can promise you that when I met God in heaven, He didn't hand me His private number. My prayers are the same as anyone else's prayers. I simply talk to Him, the same way I assume everyone else does.

What I *do* know is that the problem, at least in my life, hadn't been in talking to God—I did that just fine.

The problem was *listening* when God answered.

Before I went to heaven, I questioned God all the time. Because my life was so hard and nothing ever seemed to change for the better, I believed God wasn't listening to me or didn't care about me. My prayers felt like a one-way phone conversation, with me desperately wailing on one end, and silence on the other.

But in heaven I learned God is *always* listening. I learned He is with us every day, particularly in the dark and troubling times. This doesn't mean He will answer all our prayers the way we would like them answered. But He hears them all, and the pathway for communication between us is always open. I just tended to mistake a "no" answer as silence on God's end.

The absolute certainty I gained in heaven—that God hears us always—has made me much more attentive to what God might say in return.

And what I've come to understand is that God doesn't communicate with me through thunder and lightning. In my life, there are no booming voices, no burning bush. I realize now that God communicated with me in a series of small and beautiful ways. Of course, I didn't pick up on them all. I wasn't always paying attention. I laugh at the thought that, after trying to get my attention for so many years, God must have finally turned to my angels and said, "This one just doesn't get it. I'm literally going to have to let her die to teach her how to live."

And once God had my attention, He never, ever lost it.

One of the ways God communicates with me here on earth is through something I call a nudge.

For me, a nudge is simply a sudden instinct that overcomes me. It's an urge, a feeling, an idea that pops into my head. The way I know a certain nudge is from God is when it urges me to do something I usually *don't* want to do. For instance, there have been times when I'll be at a restaurant with Virgil and the kids, and I'll be just about to dig into my dinner when I get a nudge to tell the person sitting next to us how very much God loves them. Now, interrupting someone who is having dinner—and letting my own food get cold—is not something I want to do. In fact, I really dislike doing it. But because the nudge is so strong, and because it's something I don't want to do, I know it is a nudge from God. And so I do it.

Or, I should say, I do it most of the time. I try to do everything God tells me, but I'm certainly no saint. Sometimes I let a nudge pass. But what I've learned is that when I don't do something God asks, He doesn't stop asking. It makes me think of what Whoopi Goldberg's character experiences in the movie *Ghost*—when Patrick Swayze's ghost keeps singing "I'm Henry VIII, I Am" over and over and over again until she finally agrees to do what he asked. God doesn't sing to me, but His gentle urging is relentless. It doesn't subside until I do what He asked.

Another way God speaks to me is through my dreams. Three years before I died, I had a particularly powerful dream about my brother, Jayson. At the time, Jayson was struggling in his life. Like me, he was headstrong. Everything we'd gone through as kids had left us battered and scarred. Only instead of turning to food or long work hours to treat the despair, he drank. He was drinking too much and his faith in God was under assault. Yet in the dream, I saw my brother standing on a big stage in church, singing and leading people in worship of God. I had never seen people worship God like that before, yet there my brother was, arms raised and head thrown back, singing at the top of his lungs. The dream didn't make much sense, but I never forgot it, and over the years it brought me comfort. I held out hope that even if God wasn't going to save me, one day He would save my brother. And one day he did.

My brother gave his life to Christ in a jail cell and never looked back. He sought God, straightened up his affairs, and a few years later married the love of his life—a preacher's daughter named Melissa. Jayson has been known to get up on the stage of her family's church and leads others in the beautiful worship of God.

Ever since then, I've tried to pay very close attention to my dreams.

Beyond the nudges and the dreams, sometimes God just plants a tiny seed in my spirit. I don't always understand it at first, but over time it grows and grows and soon it overwhelms me. It starts out as the subtlest way God communicates with me. But it can also be the most powerful.

I think of it as a whisper straight to my heart.

Believe me, I get it when people say, "God, can You hear me? Are You listening?" I asked those very questions for most of my life. But now I understand that God is *always* listening, and it's up to us to open our ears and open our hearts so we can hear Him when He answers.

Pay attention to your dreams.

Be aware of the nudges.

Listen for the small, still voice inside you.

Because what you are hearing just may be a whisper from God.

CHAPTER EIGHTEEN

Leather and Grace

IN 2013, A FRIEND INVITED ME TO SPEAK AT A SMALL church in Texas. I accepted the invitation, but when I learned more about the church, I felt a little hesitant. The church was called Broken Chains, and it was known as a "biker church." In my mind I pictured a dark, smoky room filled with tattooed bikers wearing bandannas, leather jackets, boots with sharp spurs, and chains connected to their wallets hanging from their pockets. I imagined a crowd of surly bikers not laughing at any of my jokes and breaking out in a brawl at any moment. When I told Virgil about my concerns, he just laughed.

"It's a biker *church*, Crystal," he said, "not a biker *bar*."

I can laugh now, too, when I think back to my ridiculous misconceptions. Because the day I walked into Broken Chains was the day my view of what a "church" is changed forever.

I sure had an idea of what I thought church should be. For me, it was a beautiful building that was clean and inviting. Each Sunday, we would get dressed in our best clothes and be on our best behavior and sit in a pew singing hymns and listening to sermons. For most of my life, I didn't have a reason to think of church any other way.

Broken Chains changed all that.

On a hot summer evening Virgil and I drove across the Oklahoma-Texas border with our friends Brad and Wendy Pryor. We found the church just off a highway. It was a small, flat building with a sign out front that read, "Bikers Are Always Welcome Here!" Another sign showed a biker kneeling next to his motorcycle and a cross, with the inscription "All Knees Shall Bow." I took a deep breath as we pulled into the small parking lot and stopped next to a row of shiny Harleys and other bikes. I'm always nervous before I have to talk in front of a crowd, but this was way out of my comfort zone.

Inside, the church was plain and simple. There were long tables and metal chairs instead of pews, all facing a small stage toward the front. There was a small projection screen hanging off the ceiling with a message scrolling across it.

"We welcome those who feel like they are a little different or don't feel comfortable in a regular church setting. We don't care what color your skin is, what color your hair is, how many tattoos you have, how many piercings you have, or what your 'past' is. We care about your heart and where you will be spending eternity."

I thought of my own tattoos, all hidden beneath my clothes, and smiled. This might be good, I thought.

The church's pastor, Pastor Roy, came over to introduce himself. He was warm and friendly and right away I loved him. Like the building, he was much different from what I was accustomed to seeing on Sundays. While most pastors I knew wore nice suits, Pastor Roy wore blue jeans, tennis shoes, a polo shirt, and a leather vest. He definitely fit my image of a biker—a bit stocky, bushy beard, denim, and leather. He welcomed us and introduced us to some of the congregants. I was surprised to see how many families were there. Not everyone was in full biker attire; most people wore jeans and T-shirts. The atmosphere was casual, peaceful, and inviting.

We chatted with some congregants for a few minutes, then took our seats at a table near the back. The service got under way as a band went up on the small stage and began playing well-known seventies rock songs, only the lyrics were changed to words of praise and worship. They didn't have big fancy amps or expensive equipment—they just played their music loud and raw. Their passion and energy gave me goose bumps, and I swayed along to the music.

Before long, the time came for me to take the stage and share. I went to the podium, unfolded my notes, and searched my pockets for my reading glasses so I could get started.

But I couldn't find my glasses. I might have left them in my purse, in the car, or maybe even at home. All I knew was that without them, I had no hope of reading my notes. I could feel everyone staring at me, and I began to panic, which, of course, triggered my inappropriate laughter. The harder I tried to stop laughing, the more I laughed, and the more I laughed, the more people started laughing with me. Not a single one of us knew why we were laughing. Finally, I settled down enough to start my speech. The first thing I talked about was my preconceived notions about them all.

"Some of you are exactly how I pictured," I said, "but none of you are anything at all like I expected."

"Yeah, we get that a lot!" one man shouted from the back of the room.

My defenses came down, and the words began to flow. I told the story of my life and of the God Who saved it. I shared about the shame and guilt I felt over my molestation. I looked up and glimpsed a man putting his head in his hands and crying. He was one of the big biker types. Seeing this large, tough man— this beautiful intersection of grace and leather—crying for a little three-year-old girl he'd never met truly moved me.

When I finished sharing, I thanked everyone and went back to my seat. The band got back up onstage to play a few more songs. I felt my friend Brad tap me on the arm.

"I think you're needed in the back," he said.

Just a few rows behind us, a woman was bent over at the waist with her head in her lap. She was sobbing. Another woman was holding her and consoling her. I went over and sat next to the crying woman, stroked her back gently, and just listened.

Her name was Ann, and through her tears she told us how she had just gotten out of jail. She had battled addiction and lost custody of her children. She was now homeless and living in a shelter. Her tears, she explained, fell because she related to so many of the things I'd talked about in my speech. To the abuse and the feeling of being lost. Most important, she said, she knew what it felt like to wonder if God could ever love someone like her. The pain and hurt she felt inside were deeply evident as she rocked back and forth crying.

I took her hand in mine and I assured her that God *did* love her, and the reason I knew that to be true was because God loved someone like me. By then there was a small crowd of women around Ann, and we all prayed together over our new friend.

Back in Oklahoma, I couldn't get Ann out of my mind. I prayed for her often and I found that I was worrying about her a lot. Finally I called Pastor Roy, and he put me in touch with Candi, the woman who'd been consoling Ann. Candi, it turned out, volunteered at a women's shelter, teaching GED classes among many other things. I asked her how Ann was doing, and Candi let out a sigh.

"I don't know," she said, her voice heavy with sadness. "I tried to keep in touch with her, but she's no longer in the shelter and I lost track of her. I deal with women like her every day and it just breaks my heart. Some will hitchhike out of town or go back to the streets before I can help them. Sometimes I feel like they fall right through my fingers and the cracks of the system. I hate it."

I told Candi about how I'd asked God to break my heart for the things that break His, and about how deeply Ann had touched me.

"Well, if you want to help, I have hundreds more just like her," Candi said.

She told me about a ministry she runs for the homeless in her city.

"It's called Church Without Walls," she said, "and if you're praying for a broken heart, this church will break your heart *wide* open."

Candi is a little dynamo of a woman with short brown hair and a beautiful smile. She is not the kind of person who is happy with just a handshake; instead she wraps you up in a giant hug. In fact, I've never met anyone who enjoys hugging people as much as she does. Candi explains that she likes to hug people because she understands the power of human touch. Growing up, she needed a few hugs herself but rarely got them. Like when her mother died when Candi was just twelve. Her father, unable to handle the loss, withdrew from his daughter and disappeared for days and weeks at a time. Candi still remembers standing at her mother's funeral, trying to imagine what her life would look like now.

"I remember the fear I felt as I wondered where I would eat or sleep that day," Candi shared with me. "I remember feeling so alone, and that's a feeling I don't want anyone else to have to feel."

Candi grew up and became a wife, mother, and teacher. Every morning as she headed to school, she'd stop and grab a coffee at the same little store. And every morning she would buy an extra coffee for her friend Mike, who sat outside on the street. She'd spend a few minutes catching up with Mike and asking him if he needed anything. Mike never asked for anything, but he always had a funny story or joke to share. The closer Candi got to him, the more she began to worry where he slept at night and how he survived.

One morning, on her way to work, Candi didn't see Mike outside the store. A week passed and still no sign of Mike. Candi decided to leave her own world and venture into Mike's—a world she never thought she'd be a part of. Eventually she found him again, but it was the time she spent searching and meeting other homeless people that sowed the seeds for Church Without Walls.

Over time Candi developed relationships with the homeless men and women she encountered. She'd sit and listen to their stories, hold them, and pray with them. To her, they weren't bums or vagrants—they were someone's sons and daughters. The experience changed her, and she devoted herself to helping these forgotten, discarded people. What she learned in her time with them was that they felt unwelcome in church because of how they looked and the way they lived. The idea that these people couldn't know the love of God because of their appearance hurt Candi's heart. She began to think that if she couldn't bring them to church with her, maybe she could bring the church to them.

A few weeks after speaking with her, on a sunny Sunday afternoon, Virgil and I packed up our kids and drove eighty-five miles to see the church. None of us knew what to expect, and I had no answers for my teenagers when they asked me what we'd be doing at this church. The twins were only four then, and oblivious to the fact that some people lived on the streets. Virgil and I did our best to try to explain to them what it meant to be homeless, and we carefully went over some rules we wanted them to follow to be safe.

Finally we arrived at a large area below a highway overpass in the downtown region of the city. There was no stage, no pews, no pulpit, nothing—just an empty space being filled by people in tattered clothing and volunteers hauling tables and chairs out of the beds of their pickup trucks. I saw a few of the bikers I remembered from Broken Chains helping out, and I saw Candi lugging folding chairs. Suddenly I felt my stomach seize up. As much as I really wanted to do more for God in my life, I was nervous because I'd never spent any time around people who were homeless. The only time I'd even seen them, sadly, was through a car window. It wasn't that I didn't know there were needy people in the world—it was that I didn't understand how I could possibly make a difference to them.

Virgil took the twins over to a grassy area beneath the overpass where they could run and play. My older kids and I wandered around and tried to figure out what to do. I felt extremely awkward. I didn't know how to talk to "homeless people." I didn't know what to say to them. So I stayed close to the other volunteers instead. Some tables had been set up with grilled hamburgers, and a woman volunteering behind them asked if we wanted to come help serve the food. The three of us found spots behind the table and put on plastic serving gloves.

There must have been at least fifty or sixty people standing in line waiting for food. Some were young, some old, some in between. Many of them looked like they'd been living on the street for years, but others looked like they'd only recently fallen on hard times. Still others looked like any other family. Candi came over, hugged me, and thanked us for coming. She helped us hand out plates of food, and I noticed that she addressed each person in the line by name.

"Someday I want to have enough volunteers so we can sit everyone down and serve them at their tables," Candi said when we finished serving everyone. "I would love for them to know what it feels like to be served instead of having to wait in line for everything. That's my dream, anyway."

It wasn't enough for Candi to serve these people; she wanted to figure out a way to serve them *better*.

It made me think of Jesus washing the feet of His disciples. Jesus "did not come to be served," it says in Matthew 20:28, "but to serve."

After the lunch, I heard the sound of familiar rock music, with the lyrics changed to glorify God. I turned around and saw the band that had played at Broken Chains playing again. Then a tall, slender man in his early twenties got up to speak. He had bright eyes and auburn hair, and he looked young enough to be my son. In fact he was the pastor of Church Without Walls. His name was Clinton and he delivered a beautiful short sermon, though not every word was audible because of the steady roar of cars and trucks on the highway overhead.

Clinton led an altar call and I watched as he, Candi, and other volunteers embraced the people who came up for prayer. When the service was over, everyone pitched in to clean up and pack the tables away. Looking around, I realized I couldn't tell the people who were homeless from the people who were volunteers.

I wasn't the only one. A group of high school students who were volunteering rounded up the leftover hamburgers and put them in bags and handed them out to the homeless. I went to check on Virgil and the twins, and found them sitting under a tree eating hamburgers out of one of the bags. It took me a second before I realized the high school kids must have thought Virgil and the twins were homeless.

"Why did you take the burgers?" I asked Virgil.

"'Cause we're hungry," he said with a smile.

This church, I realized, wasn't just missing walls. It didn't have any judgments or distinctions, either.

And it was *exactly* the kind of church I'd been looking for my whole life.

CHAPTER NINETEEN

Two Steps Back

ON MY FIRST TRIP TO NEW YORK CITY TO VISIT with the publisher of *Waking Up in Heaven*, I met a sweet and friendly young man named Kevin. Kevin worked in the corporate offices of the publisher, in Rockefeller Center, and during my visit we had a chance to talk. He was curious about my time in heaven, and I was curious about what it's like to live in Manhattan. We only spent a few short hours together, but we really connected. When I got back to Oklahoma, I sent Kevin a friend request on Facebook.

His reply caught me completely by surprise.

"Crystal, before you accept me as your friend, I know you are a Christian and I think you should know that I'm gay," he wrote. "If you don't want to accept me on Facebook, I understand."

More than anything, Kevin's response made me feel sad. He assumed that my Christianity would prevent me from wanting to get to know him or become friends with him because of his sexual orientation. Instead of expecting me to *love* him because I am a Christian, he expected me to *reject* him.

And that broke my heart.

I wrote back to Kevin that I didn't care if he was gay or not, I was already his friend and there was nothing he could do to change that. But his response really made me think about how my Christianity was viewed in the world today. It made me aware that the title "Christian" means different things to different people—and that, to some, it isn't necessarily a positive label.

It wasn't too long after meeting Kevin that I was interviewed on the morning show *Fox & Friends*. That was the segment that led to all those nasty, hurtful online comments about my appearance and sent me into my hotel bathroom crying.

I would have been very happy to pack my bags and head back to Oklahoma after the *Fox & Friends* segment, but I couldn't—I had one more interview to do in New York City that evening. It was on a national radio show hosted by Alan Colmes, a well-known liberal political commentator. Alan's radio studio was tightly packed with equipment, with just enough room for the two of us to sit beneath a pair of hanging microphones. Alan graciously welcomed me and smiled warmly, and his kindness quickly put me at ease. But then, before the show even started, he stared right into my eyes and with a half chuckle asked me the strangest question.

"So," he said, "are you going to be one of those Christians who tells me I'm going to hell?"

Once again I was startled and heartbroken. I felt so bad that someone had done something or said something to make Alan feel that way about Christians.

"Why would anyone tell you that?" I said, my eyes watering. We were just about to go live on air, and I could feel myself beginning to hyperventilate, and Lord, I tried really hard not to cry, but I just couldn't help it. Even worse, I could see Alan felt bad about making me tear up.

"Well," he said, almost apologetically, "because I'm Jewish."

I didn't know how to react to that, so I sobbed some more and said, "My Savior was a Jew."

"Actually, I'm more of an agnostic," Alan further explained. But that didn't help, because I had no idea what "agnostic" meant.

"I was raised mostly Methodist," I said, blowing my nose and taking a sip of water. "What denomination is agnostic?"

Patiently, and through a lovely smile, Alan explained it meant he wasn't sure if there was a God.

"Alan," I said just before we went live, "I can promise you this, my friend—God is real."

My twenty-minute segment with Alan Colmes turned out to be one of the best interviews I've ever had. He was sweet, generous, and nonjudgmental, and we had an honest and meaningful conversation about God, heaven, and Christianity.

Ten months later, out of the blue, Alan called me. He had a new radio show, and he wanted me on as a guest again. This time, he gave me *a full hour* to talk about God. He even defended me when one of the callers challenged my story.

A few months later on Easter Sunday, Virgil and I were driving with the twins when we stopped for gas and saw a man, a woman, and two teenage girls sitting on a curb outside a 7-Eleven. Their clothes were clean and they looked like any other family—maybe a family having car trouble or something.

"They are homeless," Virgil said to me.

"No, they're not," I argued. "They have kids!"

Then I saw a red children's wagon filled with black trash bags next to them, and I noticed the man writing something on a piece of dirty cardboard. All at once I realized Virgil was right.

I followed my husband as he got out of the car and went over to ask the man if they needed any help. The man stood up and gave us a suspicious look. His wife and daughters had the same wide-eyed, shell-shocked expressions.

"It's okay," I assured them. "We are Christians."

I thought that maybe the mother hadn't heard me, because when I said "Christians" she pulled her girls close to her and took two steps back.

Here it was, happening *again*—someone recoiling at the mention of the word *Christian*. Someone stepping away from me instead of toward me. Why?

Virgil and I listened as the father told us his story—he had recently lost his job, then his car, then his house. All they owned now was what they had managed to stuff into the black trash bags.

"It all happened so quickly," the father said, shaking his head.

We stayed with them for an hour, talking and sharing and praying. Then Virgil arranged for them to stay in a nearby hotel. He also gave them information about agencies in the city that might help the father get back on his feet. The father stuck out his hand and met Virgil in a firm handshake.

"Happy Easter," he said.

"Happy Easter, friend," Virgil replied.

Just as we were walking away, the mother rushed over and gave me a big hug.

"Thank you for not judging us," she said.

I understood exactly what she meant. The truth is, for much of my life I *had* judged people like her. The reality of who they are—human beings with hard lives and tough problems—didn't move me enough to go out of my way and do something to help. It is painful to think back to that time and admit the truth, but the fact is I didn't care enough about them to take any action besides saying a quick prayer.

It was through my experiences with Kevin and Alan Colmes and the family on Easter Sunday that I learned a truly valuable lesson: the importance of asking ourselves, "What kind of Christian am I?"

It's not a question I ever spent much time thinking about. To me, a Christian is someone who follows Christ; who is charitable and giving; who reads the Bible and heeds the word of God. Being a Christian means being someone who is *good*.

Yet the *perception* of Christians in the world today is not nearly that simple or straightforward. A recent study by the Barna Group explored this very question: How well do "Christians seem to emulate the actions and attitudes of Christ in their interactions with others"? The report's findings were shocking—more than half of the Christians who participated in the study exhibited actions and attitudes that were more self-righteous

than Christ-like. Only 14 percent of those studied exhibited behavior "consistent with that of the Lord."

Is it possible Christians are becoming better known for what
they stand against than what they stand *for?*

For much of my life I claimed to be a Christian, yet I never
lived or even tried to live as He instructed. His message is simple
and beautiful—He says to love others as He loves us. But if all
I do as a Christian is judge and ridicule and condemn, how will
that ever make someone want to know the Lord I love so much?
Did my behavior ever hurt someone, the way Kevin and Alan
and the family were hurt by critical comments and actions? Were
there times when I didn't love others the way He wants me to
love them?

And even after all of my earthly sins, God wrapped me in His
love in heaven. He didn't judge me—instead He bathed me in
forgiveness. But how can others come to know the Lord's magnificent love unless we as Christians show it to them?

In heaven, God told me to share my story with the world. And
since I came back, it hasn't been lost on me that God has steered
me mainly toward secular audiences. Yes, I tell my story in
churches, but much more often I tell it at women's events, at book
clubs, at pregnancy resource centers—and on nonreligious TV
and radio shows where there's such a thing as talking *too* much
about God.

The lesson I've learned is that it *matters* how I project my
Christianity to the world. It *matters* that I actively fight against
the assumptions and preconceptions of what being a Christian

means. Going forward, I will always be aware of what my words and actions convey and how they reflect my true, core beliefs. I will never apologize for my faith, nor will I ever miss a chance to spread God's Word everywhere I go. But at every stop I will try to change people's perceptions of what Christianity means, if their perceptions are anything less than us being God's loving messengers.

But first I had to ask myself two hard questions:

What kind of Christian am I?

And what kind of Christian do I want to be?

CHAPTER TWENTY

Bank Robbers and Baptisms

M Y FAMILY AND I KEPT GOING TO CHURCH WITH-
out Walls once a month. Each time we were there, it became
easier for us to find our place. Whatever judgments I'd made about
the homeless in the past had fallen away, replaced by the reality of
what I saw under the overpass.

It was especially hard for Virgil when he realized just how
many of the homeless population were military veterans. Many
had been leading normal, ordinary lives— holding jobs, raising kids, buying houses—until a bad break or a bad decision
knocked them off course. Many were fighting battles against
addiction or mental illness. Some were sick and couldn't work
and had no one to help them get by. Some literally lived on the
streets—in alleys and doorways and parks—while others were
staying in shelters, low-income government housing, or nursing
homes.

It got to where we stopped seeing these people as "homeless" and began thinking of them as just friends.

The stories they told were powerful and heartbreaking. One man, Stephen, lived behind a Dumpster in an alley. Over the years Candi brought him blankets and food and became his friend. But like so many others Candi had met, Stephen seemed incapable of making any big or drastic changes in his life. So Candi vowed simply to love him just as—and where—he was.

Then Candi heard Stephen had been hit by a car and left to die alone on the side of a road. She was distraught. Stephen had no family or friends, so his body went unclaimed. It was Candi and Candi alone who stood in the cemetery as Stephen's remains were placed in an unmarked grave.

Another man I met, Butch, was in his early fifties. Butch spent most nights sleeping under a tarp, but he refused to stay in a shelter because he didn't want to leave his only companion—a scruffy little dog named Kato. The second I sat down to talk with Butch, I immediately recognized he was a kind, gentle, and giving soul. Like a lot of our friends on the streets, he battled a daily addiction. Candi stepped in and promised to take care of Kato, which allowed Butch to go into rehab. That decision changed his life. Butch got a job and his own small apartment, with a special little dog bed just for Kato.

I met two deaf brothers in their sixties who were both homeless and stuck close together so they could help each other survive. Communicating wasn't easy, but I spent time with them laughing, joking, and sharing a little bit of life together. Then the brothers disappeared, and it's been months since I've seen them. I pray for them often and I hope that the world is being kind to them.

And then there's Castro, a sweet man in his seventies with few to no teeth and a shopping cart filled with all his earthly possessions. A year after I met him, my friend Erin, who is fluent in Spanish, spoke with him. She turned to me and said, "His name isn't Castro, it's Luis!" Castro, it turned out, was the nickname the guys on the street gave him because he was from Cuba.

"When I turn seventy-three," Luis proudly told me in his badly broken English, "I am going back to heaven." And he pointed up into the sky.

I smiled and said, "You will love it, friend. It is beautiful."

Toward the fall, as the temperatures began to drop, I asked Candi what I could do to help our friends on the streets. She told me they always needed coats and blankets. I put out the request on our Facebook page, and before long I had bag after bag of donated items outside my front door. One woman drove ninety minutes just to drop off six bags filled with nearly brand-new clothing she wanted us to have.

The generosity of so many people made me want to cry. But another donation stopped me in my tracks.

It was several bags of clothing donated by a small church a few towns away. I opened the first bag and dumped the clothes in the middle of my living room to sort through them. As I did, I gasped in disgust. The clothes were stained, ripped, and filthy. The shirts were torn and worn out while the shoes had giant holes in them. There were used socks and underwear. The next five bags had more of the same.

"Help us show the love of the Lord," I'd written on Facebook in my call for action.

And as I stood beside the pile of dirty clothing I thought, *This is what they think the love of our Savior looks like?*

And very kindly God reminded me that, not too long ago, this was what *I* thought the love of our Savior looked like.

Before I met God, I was the one who filled up trash bags with stuff I no longer wanted and dropped them off at the Goodwill in town. I knew that what was in those bags probably belonged in the garbage, but I convinced myself that there was value in what I was doing. "Beggars can't be choosers," I thought.

Now I felt ashamed that I'd ever accepted that giving in this manner in any way represents the Lord.

I sat down and prayed, asking God to forgive me. I changed the wording of my post on Facebook.

"New or like-new clothing items, shoes, and blankets," I wrote. "If you wouldn't give it to God, let's not give it to represent Him, either."

It was a message I needed to hear as much as anyone else.

The donations kept pouring in. Toothpaste, wet wipes, soaps, and nonperishable food—my home began to look like a warehouse. Virgil and the kids helped me put the supplies into little bags we could hand out to our friends on the streets. We called them Love Bags—for "Love others, value everyone." On some Sundays, we'd hand out as many as fifty or sixty Love Bags. Eventually, I heard that other families were assembling Love Bags with their kids and handing them out, too.

Last Christmas, we decided we wanted to hand out gifts to our friends on the streets on Christmas Eve. Pastor Clinton immediately dropped all his plans and agreed to come with us. Clinton and Candi were out on the streets just about every day, and

Clinton knew where we should go to find people. We followed him as he led us to back alleys, abandoned homes, and Dumpsters. When we found a friend, we'd all sit with them and give them a wrapped Christmas present. Most of them told us it was the only Christmas gift they would get.

One man looked at his gift, a red winter hat, and tried to offer us the only thing in the world he had to offer—the doughnut someone had recently given him to eat.

We began taking Love Bags with us wherever we went, in case we ran into someone in need. One day we drove past a man sitting alongside a busy intersection in the pouring rain, holding a sign that asked for help. Virgil pulled over, ran across the intersection, and sat down next to the man. The twins and I watched as another man approached them. After talking to the two men for a while, Virgil joined hands with them and prayed. Then my husband gave them each a bag and a hug.

"Do you see your daddy over there?" I asked the twins as the rain drenched Virgil and the homeless men. "That is what the hands and feet of our Savior look like."

Micah and Willow didn't understand. But I hoped that through their father's example of unconditional love for the least of us, one day they would understand.

After Virgil got back in the car, it took him a second to speak.

"They were both veterans," he said.

Prayer is a very powerful tool, but it's even more powerful when coupled with service. Especially for a person who hasn't eaten for three days.

Shane Claiborne put it so well when he said, "How can we worship a homeless man on Sunday and ignore one on Monday?"

In Matthew 25:35–40, Jesus tells His followers:

"For I was hungry and you gave Me something to eat, I was thirsty and you gave Me something to drink, I was a stranger and you invited Me in, I needed clothes and you clothed Me, I was sick and you looked after Me, I was in prison and you came to visit Me."

Then the righteous will answer him, "Lord, when did we see You hungry and feed You, or thirsty and give You something to drink? When did we see You a stranger and invite You in, or needing clothes and clothe You? When did we see You sick or in prison and go to visit you?"

The King will reply, "Truly I tell you, whatever you did for one of the least of these brothers and sisters of Mine, you did for Me."

The Lord was instructing us to care for the sick and the needy, the hungry and the thirsty, the poor and the addicted, the impoverished and imprisoned. He was calling us to love them as He loved us. Before I went to heaven, I failed to live up to what God asked of me, and even after I returned from heaven I have often come up short. I am human, and I make plenty of mistakes and miss plenty of opportunities to love. I still struggle, every single day. But that is the beautiful thing about our Savior—while we struggle and fail, His love for us never does.

He whispers, "Keep going, keep trying, keep learning."

During the warmer months, Candi and the volunteers at Church Without Walls include baptisms in their Sunday services. They fill an old metal horse trough with water and welcome anyone who wants to be baptized. One Sunday I was at the church for a baptismal service with my friend from back home, Sarah. Sarah had been coming with me for about a year, and I could tell that the experience had changed her. When we saw the horse trough filled with water, Sarah grabbed my arm.

"I want to be baptized today," she said.

Sarah and I had been friends for years and shared just about everything with each other. One night we sat in my car having a heart-to-heart conversation, and we talked about a friend of ours who had recently discovered her husband was unfaithful. We talked about how much pain our friend was in, and I thought back to when I was younger, when I played a part in the breakup of a marriage.

"I hurt so many people," I told Sarah, my heart bursting with remorse. "I am so sorry for the pain I caused and for the person I used to be."

Sarah squeezed my hand and said, "Crystal, we all make mistakes. Um—I robbed a bank."

I looked at her in disbelief. "You did *what?*"

She took a deep breath and told me her own story.

Several years earlier, Sarah was in an abusive marriage with a domineering man. She worked as a teller in a bank, and over time her husband pushed her into stealing small amounts of money. She felt a horrible sense of guilt, and she never spent any of the money herself, but she wasn't strong enough to stand up to her husband. Eventually her shame got so bad, Sarah turned herself in. She was charged with a felony, paid restitution, and was put on parole.

After that Sarah left her husband and built a brand-new life. She married a good man in the military, and today they have three kids. Talking about her past, Sarah didn't feel sorry for herself or try to explain away her actions. She just made it clear she was a very different person now. It's easy for me to see the many ways she's changed, and she is always there with me to help those who need it—making Love Bags, raising donations, and passing out presents on the streets.

And now, at Church Without Walls, she wanted to rededicate herself to the Lord.

I looked at the line of people waiting to be baptized at the horse trough, and I smiled.

Perfect, I thought. *Homeless people, drug addicts, and now a bank robber. I'm right where I belong.*

When it was Sarah's turn, I helped her step into the trough, blue jeans and all. She asked if I would baptize her, and I told her I'd be honored.

"Sarah, do you know that the Lord loves you?" I asked as I knelt beside her.

"Yes, I do," she said.

"Do you know that Jesus died to pay the price for your sins so you can live forever with Him in heaven?"

"Yes, I do," she said.

"Do you accept Him as your Lord and Savior?"

"Yes," Sarah said, tears spilling from her eyes.

"Then, my friend, I baptize you in the name of Jesus and our Father in Heaven."

Sarah went under the water, and came up drenched in love.

Afterward I drove my soaking-wet friend to a nearby Target so she could buy some dry jammies to wear home. In the store her sneakers squeaked with water and she left a series of puddles behind her, but she didn't care, and neither did I.

Sarah's baptism was one of the most inspiring moments I'd ever been part of, but it wasn't even the most inspiring thing I saw at Church Without Walls that day.

During the service, Pastor Clinton began to offer communion. Willow looked up at me and asked, "What's communion?" Virgil knelt down in front of her and explained the symbolism of the body and blood of Christ.

"Can we have it?" Micah asked.

"Of course you can," Virgil said.

The twins waited until Pastor Clinton came around to them, and then they opened their small hands and took the little squares of bread. There was no big ceremony, no celebration in front of all our friends and family, no curriculum or questions to answer. It was just my babies saying, "Yes, we love You, Jesus." The same Jesus Who had said, "Let the little children come to Me."

It was their First Communion.

And at that moment I looked around me once more—at the folding chairs and tables, at the bikers in boots and leather jackets handing out hot dogs and chili, at Butch, Kato, Luis, and all the other friends I'd made, at the bare ground that served as our floor and the concrete pillars that served as our borders, at Candi baptizing people in the old horse trough, at my daughter Sabyre singing with the band, at Micah and Willow running happily back to us—and I had a thought, a clear, wonderful, beautiful thought.

This, I thought, *is my favorite church.*

My time in heaven—and the unforgettable moment when God showed me my three-year-old self—taught me that we are all

God's perfect children and that we are all perfectly worthy of His love. Not just some of us—*all* of us. God loves us all with a glorious, burning, passionate love that I was blessed to be able to feel in a way I'd never felt before. And if God could love me—a sinner, a judger, a skeptic—I know that He can and He does love *all* His children. How far we fall, how dirty we get—none of that matters in the slightest.

What matters is that God loves us, and we are worthy of His love.

It's like what Pastor Roy wrote on the Broken Chains website:

"God cares more about the condition of your heart than your outer appearance."

Every year in America, about a thousand new churches get built. But each year, about *four* thousand churches close their doors. In the 1980s, membership in Christian churches dropped almost 10 percent. The next decade, the decline was 12 percent. In the last twenty years, the numbers are even worse. According to some studies, millions of young people stop going to church each year. Most of them think church is irrelevant. One Christian minister concluded, "They put God on the back burner."

More and more people today are not finding God in the church.

I can understand that. Being in heaven taught me to look for God in places I'd never searched before. And in the end, I didn't find God in a bright, beautiful church building that summer.

Instead I found Him right there in the dirt.

———————— 🐦 ————————

CHAPTER TWENTY-ONE

The Breath of Jesus

THE WORKDAY WAS JUST GETTING STARTED AT A dentist's office in Mangum, a small Oklahoma town about half an hour from where I live. Three patients were already in the office, waiting to be seen. But the hygienist was late, and in twenty years of working there she had almost never been late. The dentist remembered seeing a sheriff's patrol car by the side of the road on his way to work, and with a sickening feeling in his stomach, he picked up the phone to call the sheriff's office and ask if there'd been any accidents that morning.

The sheriff said yes, there had been an accident on Route 62.

The dentist hung up and asked another staffer to drive out to the site of the crash to see who'd been involved.

Around the same time that morning, I was in a car with my friend Sarah, driving to Oklahoma City to get birth certificates for her kids. We had stopped for coffee, and now we were about to get on the turnpike. My cell phone rang, and I saw it was my mother's work number.

"What's up, Mom?" I asked cheerfully.

"Crystal?" someone other than my mother answered.

My heart skipped a beat.

"It's Madison," the woman said. Madison was the receptionist at the dentist's office where my mom worked. "Has anyone told you about your mom?"

My body went numb. Involuntarily I began to lightly hit Sarah, who was driving, on the arm. I felt my throat seize up and my stomach clench with dread. I felt so weak that even the phone seemed heavy in my hand.

"Wh-what happened?" I managed to stammer.

I can barely remember what Madison told me next. But I do remember screaming, and repeatedly yelling the same two words at Sarah as my taps on her shoulder became more panicked.

"*Turn around!*"

The drive to work in her white SUV was always my mother's quiet time. She liked to listen to praise-and-worship music on the radio, and she used the thirty-minute commute to talk to God. She'd recently injured her shoulder in a fall, and when she got up that morning she expected it to hurt, but was happily surprised when it didn't.

"Thank you for taking the pain away today," she said to God as she drove.

She stopped at an intersection on Route 62 and flicked on her left turn signal. All she had to do was drive across the highway and in a mile or two she would be at work. She had made this drive—this turn—thousands of times before. She looked up and saw another driver coming down the highway toward her, but he had his right turn signal on. The driver was getting off at the intersection, too. Slowly, my mother turned left and started driving across the highway.

But the other driver didn't turn right—and he didn't slow down.

Instead of turning, he kept driving straight at sixty-five miles per hour. His car smashed directly into the passenger side of my mother's SUV.

Both cars spun and screeched to a stop off the road. My mother's airbag blew open. The crash made a horrifying sound, but within seconds there was nothing but an eerie silence on the highway. That, and scattered chunks of metal and glass.

Inside the SUV, my mother couldn't move.

"We have detected there has been an accident," the voice from her OnStar speaker intoned. "Are you okay?"

"No," my mother whispered, pain radiating through her body. "I'm not okay. I'm hurt badly. Please call my daughter."

Within moments passersby rushed to the mangled cars to help. A MedFlight helicopter was called to take my mom to a hospital an hour away.

The very same hospital where, six years earlier, I had died.

Sarah drove us to the hospital with her hazard lights on, going as fast as she legally could. My hands were shaking as I called my younger brother, Jayson, who lives in Ohio. I had almost no information to give him, but he immediately said he was on his way. One of my mom's coworkers had gone to the scene of the accident, but all she could tell me when she called was that the crash had been "really bad."

"Crystal," she said, "I put my hand on her as they were putting her in the helicopter and told her she wasn't alone. I told her she was loved and I prayed."

"Did she speak to you?" I asked. "Was she scared?"

"She asked me to call you," she said.

I prayed all the way to the hospital, pleading to God, over and over, "Please let her be okay. Please let her live."

I was the first family member to get to the hospital. I ran through the ER looking for someone who could tell me what was happening. A staffer told me my mother had just arrived on the helicopter, and someone would give me information as soon as possible. I tried sitting in the waiting room, but every few minutes I'd jump up and ask a different nurse if they knew anything. None of them did.

Forty-five minutes later, I finally saw members of the hospital's flight team walking down the hall. I ran over and caught up to them.

"Are you from the car accident?" I asked.

"Yes," one of them said.

"She's my mother. How is she?"

He looked at me and in a somber voice said, "She has a lot of broken bones. But she is alert."

For the first time since I got the call from Madison, I knew my mother was still alive.

A nurse finally came out to the waiting room and called me back. I learned just how badly broken my mother was. She had a deep, purple laceration across her torso from where her seat belt had pressed into her. Both of her legs were broken, as were most of her ribs. Mom had a closed head injury, and her right shoulder was completely shattered—the same shoulder she'd thanked God for healing earlier that day.

As I walked toward my mother's room, I asked the nurse if any other bones had been broken. Without a word, she nodded and pointed to her back.

"Oh my gosh," I said.

Barely able to catch my breath, I walked into my mom's room. Her eyes were closed and she was hooked up to monitors and machines.

"Mom, I'm here," I whispered as I bent over and kissed her head. Her neck was in a brace, which made it impossible for her to turn toward me. I leaned across her so that she could see me.

"Well, your makeup is perfect," I said with a giggle. "You look beautiful."

My mother, a devoted cosmetic consultant, smiled weakly and said, "Because it's Mary Kay."

Smiling, I said, "You know, if you didn't feel like babysitting for my anniversary tonight, there were easier ways to get out of it."

Later, I said, "Mom, I swear to you, I didn't step on a crack."

But the most important thing I said to her was, "Mom, I love you so much."

My mother spent the next thirteen hours in the emergency room. Four different types of doctors were called in to treat her. The doctors performed scan after scan, trying to figure out what else was wrong with her. They were especially worried about internal injuries and the three breaks they found in her back. Remarkably, I didn't see any huge lacerations or much blood coming from her wounds. The doctors explained that that didn't mean she wasn't bleeding internally.

After all the tests and scans were done, the doctors moved my mother to the intensive care unit. I set up shop in the corner of her room, unwilling to leave her side. By then my brother, Jayson, and his wife, Melissa, had arrived.

"Let me get this straight," Jayson said to our mom, his voice breaking with emotion. "With what could have been your dying breath, you asked for Crystal?" Then he smiled and teased, "I guess we all know who your favorite is now."

Virgil was at the hospital, too. His mother had driven down from Oklahoma City to stay with the twins. Two days after the crash, my mother had major surgery on the broken bones in one of her legs. No one could tell us anything definitive about her condition. All we knew for sure was that she was in terrible pain.

That first night in the ICU, I sat in the corner of her room and prayed. My mother was hooked up to a morphine drip, and for the most part she was incoherent. Occasionally I reached over and touched some part of her body.

That's when it occurred to me—we had switched positions.

Six years earlier, in the very same hospital, it had been my mother at the foot of my bed, and me hooked up to a pain pump, and my mother touching me and telling me I would be okay, and me smiling weakly and drifting in and out of consciousness.

It was my mother who was there at the foot of my bed when I stopped breathing and a nurse hollered, "Code Blue!" and doctors burst into the room and tried to bring me back to life. It was my mother who had to watch a doctor straddle my body and pound on my chest. My mother likes to say that my nine minutes in heaven were her nine minutes in hell. But it was only then, as I sat at the foot of *her* bed, that I truly realized how terrible those moments had been for her.

All of a sudden, one of my mother's monitors went off.

It went from a gentle hum to a loud alarm. A nurse rushed in and tried to talk to my mom, but she was becoming unresponsive. Another nurse checked my mother's vital signs and saw that they were dropping. I watched in horror as the hospital room filled up with nurses and doctors, and I heard someone say, "We might have to intubate her." The monitors were going crazy now, and my mom's vital signs kept dropping. I watched her breathing get really shallow, as if she was struggling to breathe.

Six years earlier my mother had watched me die.

Now it was me watching her slip away.

The night before the car crash, I was at home sitting on the sofa and wearing a beauty treatment mud mask. I took a picture of myself with the green goo and texted it to my mom. Beneath it I typed, "There's a supermodel under here." A bit later my cell rang, and it was her calling. She liked to call me most evenings, just to catch up. But that night, I was tired and had my mud mask on, so I texted my mom and told her I couldn't talk. She texted me back and said, "Okay, talk soon. I love you."

I didn't take my mother's call because I didn't want to mess up my beauty mask.

The next morning, she was in the accident.

In the hospital, my mom's vital signs continued to drop. Her breathing got more and more labored. Her lung had collapsed, and that made drawing even one breath hard for her. A doctor told us they believed the effects of the pain medication were making her breathing worsen. I saw a doctor preparing a big needle to inject in my mother's arm. I knew what was in that needle. It was Narcan, a drug that instantly blocks painkillers from reaching the body's pain sensors. It was the very same drug the doctors administered to me when I died. As I watched the doctor inject her, I welled up with tears. I remembered how incredibly painful it was to suddenly have all your painkillers stop working. I knew that my mom was about to feel every last one of her broken bones.

The Narcan did its job, and my mother's breathing became less labored. She was able to talk, but only a little—just a word or two. Her vital signs slowly crept in the right direction. For the moment, my mother's condition had stabilized.

But she wasn't out of the woods. The doctors explained that their biggest worry was that she might have a pulmonary embolism, which is a blood clot that travels to the lungs and creates a blockage of the main artery. An embolism in her lung could easily kill her, and when he spoke to us, the doctor was extremely clear about that.

Suddenly I felt the weight of it all pressing down on me, and I burst into sobs. My brother tried to console me and asked me to tell him what I was feeling, but I couldn't talk. The girl who never shut up her entire life literally could not speak.

Images began flashing in my mind. I saw my mother laughing as I blew my first bubble, and I saw her cheering me on at a dance recital. I pictured her running beside my bike as she let go and watched me ride. I could see her sitting at her sewing machine and making my Halloween costume. I saw her at every school event, every sporting event, every holiday, every birthday. I saw her picking me up off the ground when I cut open my leg when I was eight, and holding me when I was seventeen and telling her I was pregnant. My whole life with my mother was unspooling in my mind and I couldn't make it stop. I collapsed in a chair in the waiting room and silently prayed to God.

"God, I will do anything if she can stay with me longer," I prayed. "I am not ready to lose her. I need her here with me."

It was just like the prayer my mother said when it was me who was dying.

My brother left me alone for a while, then came over and sat next to me. I was still crying so hard my body was shuddering.

"Crystal, it is going to be okay," my brother said. "The greatest thing I have to hold on to is the fact that if we lose her, heaven will gain her. To know she'd be with the Lord and no longer suffering here helps me to find comfort in all of this."

"Shut up!" I screamed out. "Don't say that! I don't want her to be with Him. I want her here with us."

I had been to heaven, but I wasn't there anymore, and I didn't want my mother to be there, either.

I know, I know—that doesn't make much sense. Why would I want so desperately for my mother to live if I knew the place she was going to was magnificent beyond words? Like I mentioned earlier, this is something I have grappled with since coming back from heaven. I do not want people who are dying to be afraid. I want them to know that what awaits them is more glorious than we can even imagine. I have felt the pull of heaven, and I know how powerful it is, and I feared my mother would feel the same pull and not want to stay here on earth.

But even though I knew full well that Jayson was right—that my mother would be with God and her suffering would end—I *still* didn't want to lose her. The thought of not having her around was simply too painful. I love my mother. And so I pulled as hard as I could for her to stay with me . . .

That night, my brother and I sat with our mom in the hospital room, just the three of us—just as it had been for most of our lives. Mom was hooked up to a machine that was helping her breathe. I held her hand and looked at her as she fell in and out of sleep. Her nightly nurse, Trina, kept coming in and out of the room, attending to different things. She was in her fifties, and had a kind face and long, graying black hair. She noticed me crying and started to talk, then got quiet. She seemed uneasy, as if she needed to tell me something but didn't quite know how. Finally she walked over and stood in front of me and braced herself.

Softly she said, "I died from what they believe your mother has."

I was stunned. I just looked at her without saying anything. She paused, then went on.

"I know that sounds crazy, but it's the truth," she said. "It was almost ten years ago. I had back surgery. I developed blood clots in my lungs, and it was very serious. I remember lying in my hospital bed, and my family was there, and I went in and out of consciousness, and even when I was awake I couldn't speak. But I had a very clear thought—I knew I wasn't doing very well. I was aware of everything that was going on around me and I could hear the doctors telling my family I probably wasn't going to make it."

Just then, Trina told me, she became aware of a doctor standing behind her hospital bed. The doctor put his hand on her shoulder, just above her chest. "I remember the way he smelled," she said. "He smelled so beautiful. More beautiful than anything I'd ever known."

"You're going to be okay," the doctor assured her.

They took Trina to the MRI room and lay her on the table. Trina couldn't speak, but her thought was, *If I lay down flat, I will code. I can't breathe if they lay me back.* That's when the mysterious doctor assured her for a second time.

"I will be there with you," he said, "and I will breathe for you."

"It was in that exact moment, as I went into the machine, that I stopped breathing," Trina said. "But then I heard the doctor whisper again that he would breathe for me and everything was going to be okay. And then . . ."

Trina trailed off, her eyes filling with tears.

"I'm not really sure how to explain this to you," she went on, "but the doctor laid his chest on top of mine and his lungs intertwined with mine and as I stopped breathing he began to breathe for me."

I felt chills run from the top of my head to the bottom of my feet.

"I knew in that moment," Trina said, "that this was not a doctor in that small space with me. It was Jesus. He was with me in the tube."

Trina felt obliged to tell me that up to that point she hadn't been particularly religious. "I didn't lead a Jesusy life," is how she put it. Nevertheless, in that moment, "all of the shame and guilt of my life came to the surface," she said, "and I begged the Lord to forgive me. I said, 'Please, please forgive me for the way I lived my life.' And He said to me, 'You are the only one who sees yourself that way. I see you as perfect and beautiful.'"

That was the point in her story when I began to weep.

I wept because *God showed me the exact same thing in heaven!* He showed me that I was His perfect and beautiful child! And He took away my shame and guilt, just like the Lord did for Trina in the MRI tube!

"Then He told me, 'You have more to do here,'" Trina continued, "and that's when I knew I wasn't going to die."

My mother's monitors purred quietly in the background. Trina exhaled and seemed almost sheepish.

"I don't share this story with many people," she said, as if apologizing. "Practically no one."

"Why not?" I asked, though I already knew the answer.

"Well, it's not an easy thing for people to believe. I have lost friends because I simply wasn't the same person after this happened. People think I'm crazy, or a liar."

"Because you can't go back to the life you had before," I said.

"Yes, that's right," Trina said, a bit surprised. "Because I can't go back to the life I had." Then she said, "All I know is that I felt like I was supposed to tell you my story. I know it sounds completely crazy, and I know it is very hard to believe."

"My friend," I said, "it's not hard for me to believe at all."

I looked at my mother, still struggling to breathe, and I prayed for the Lord to breathe for her and fill her lungs with His breath, the breath of life.

When I was in heaven, all I wanted to do was stay in heaven. When I was with God, all I wanted was to be with Him forever. When my brother told me the worst that could happen was my mother being with our Savior, he was right. I understood the beauty and glory and majesty of what awaited her. I knew she was headed to heaven.

And yet I didn't want to let her go.

"Tell them what you can remember," God commanded me. And though it took me a while, I finally realized what God was telling me.

He was telling me I had a role to play here on earth.

It was the same message the Lord had for Trina in the MRI tube—"You have more to do here."

It is the same message our Savior has for *all* of us.

We *all* have work to do here. There is no such thing as an unimportant or meaningless life. Each and every one of us is here for a reason. I later learned that the nurse who told me her story in the ICU didn't actually work in the hospital full-time. She was a traveling nurse who on that day happened to be assigned to that hospital, and serendipitously happened to be assigned to my mother's room. Some would say her presence in that room was completely random, but I don't believe it was.

I believe God sent her to minister to me at the exact moment I needed it most.

Hearing Trina's story was profoundly moving. More than anything, it was *affirming*—of life, God, His undying love for us. Once again, God tracked me down and found a way to remind me of His grace and wisdom.

He did it by *using* someone for His glory.

God has roles for us all—He has work He needs us to do. God works *through* us all the time, every single day. Sometimes we won't be happy or comfortable in our role. Trina, for instance, didn't like sharing her story because she didn't want people to think she was crazy. I understood that as well as anyone. I felt the same way, at least in the beginning. I even stopped telling my story altogether, because I couldn't take another eye roll or shake of the head. But over time I came to realize I had a calling, whether or not it made me comfortable. And so today I share my story whenever I can.

"For it is God Who works in you to will and to act in order to fulfill His good purpose," it says in Philippians 2:13.

When I died I learned that heaven is our true home. But that doesn't mean our time on earth doesn't have meaning—far from it. I faced the prospect of death head-on when I nearly lost my son in the motorcycle accident. I dealt with it again when my mother was in her horrendous car accident. And each time, I prayed harder than I'd ever prayed before, and what I prayed for was *life*. More *life*. I want my loved ones to be alive and with me here on this earth.

Even though I went to heaven and felt indescribable joy and peace, I still want to be alive right here, on this imperfect planet.

Because, I now understand, we can find God and heaven here, too.

Two days after my mother's monitors went haywire, her vital signs began to stabilize. There was no pulmonary embolism, and she started breathing on her own.

Her road back to health, however, was going to be hard. Very hard. The damage to her shoulder, in particular, was severe. She stayed in the hospital for three months before she was strong enough to come home. Since we still lived near each other, I went to see her every day. Sometimes we'd go shopping or out to lunch, with my mother leaning hard on her walker.

One day we passed by an elderly woman who was using a walker, too.

"I got five bucks that says you can't beat her in a race," I whispered to my mom with a wink. "Go on."

"Make it ten," my mother said.

Today, my mom is doing okay. She is walking better, and the range of motion in her shoulder has improved a bit. It was hard for her to accept the fact that she may never regain the full use of her shoulder, and she still has bad days where everything hurts, and she probably always will. But from where I'm sitting, there are no bad days.

There are only days I get to spend with my mom.

CHAPTER TWENTY-TWO

Because I Knew You

IT WAS MIDNIGHT WHEN WE SAID GOOD-BYE TO our husbands and our children and set out into the dark. There were three of us in the Ford Explorer—Noreen, Melba, and me. Virgil stood in the driveway and prayed over us as we drove away.

"God, protect these women," he said aloud. "Be with them on their journey."

Then we were off, through the dim, empty streets of our town, past the desolate downtown outskirts, and onto Route 44, toward Oklahoma City.

We were three friends going to see a fourth friend who needed us—two states, six hundred miles, and ten hours away.

And we were racing against the clock.

Her name is Wendy, and I would say she is my best friend, but the truth is she is everyone's best friend. She is one of those people who can brighten your life and fill up your heart just by cracking a joke when you need it most. She is originally from England and moved to Oklahoma many years ago, and she speaks with an English accent mixed with a little bit of Okie. She is a tiny thing with short hair and a giant personality. We met for the first time at a soccer match in which my young daughter Sabyre and her young son, Robert, were both playing. She pulled her folding lawn chair up next to mine, and that was that—friends for life.

The thing about Wendy is that she is outrageously giving. She is an amazing, godly wife to her husband, Richard, a military contractor, and an equally amazing mother to Robert, their only child. But Wendy's love is so expansive, there is plenty of it to go around. For instance, she loves buying presents for my children. And not just little knickknacks—gifts like a flat-screen TV for Payne and an electric guitar for Sabyre.

"Where did *that* come from?" I asked Payne when I walked into his bedroom and saw the television.

"Aunt Wendy," he said matter-of-factly, as if everyone's aunt were that generous.

Put simply, Wendy loved giving people presents. You had to be careful when you visited her home, because if you said you liked something, chances were she would buy it for you.

"These are *so* delicious," I told her as I ate some ridiculously good french fries she and Richard had made.

The next day I found a brand-new FryDaddy cooker on my front porch.

And my twins—Wendy *adored* my twins. Virgil and I didn't have to buy any outfits for Micah and Willow for a whole year because Wendy bought us so much clothing for them. Then she spoiled them with gifts and toys from Walmart.

"Wendy, we're good," I would tell her over and over. "You don't have to buy them any more stuff."

"Okay," Wendy would say. "What size pants does Willow wear?"

Beyond the presents, Wendy was a constant presence in our lives. She helped my family in any and every way that she possibly could. When I was pregnant, she picked up my older kids from school, and after I had the twins, she came over to help me feed and cuddle them. Every Friday night, we would go together to watch the high school football game—or rather, the high school band, in which Payne played trumpet and Robert played flute. On cold nights, we huddled together under a blanket and talked about a million things, not paying a bit of attention to the game. When someone scored a touchdown and the crowd around us stood up and cheered, we'd rise to our feet and yell, too, only we had no idea what we were cheering for. We were too busy making each other laugh to actually follow the game.

In this world, there are takers and there are givers.

Wendy is a giver.

When Wendy told us that she and her family would be moving to Mississippi, I was devastated. I knew it was the right choice for her, but I couldn't imagine a life without her in it.

Three years after I came back from heaven, I was checking my emails one day and saw a note from a woman who worked with Wendy. I opened it and read it, then I read it again because it didn't make any sense.

"I don't know if you know this yet," the friend wrote, "but Wendy is in the ER. We believe she had a stroke."

I was momentarily paralyzed with shock. The email didn't say much more than that, so all I knew was that something bad had happened to Wendy—and that I wanted to be with her and tell her she would be okay. I fought the instinct to grab a suitcase and set out for Mississippi right then and there. Then I reasoned that Wendy would need her friends more in the coming weeks than she did right in that moment when there was little I could do. I took several deep breaths and called our friend Noreen to find out what she knew.

"Yes, Wendy had a stroke," Noreen confirmed, her voice somber and shaky. "They're going to be moving her to another hospital."

Every instinct in my body told me to run to Wendy's side right away. Instead we decided to stay in constant contact with Richard. "Let's find out more," Noreen and I told each other. "And let's pray."

But the next day Noreen called me crying.

"Crystal, it's not good," she said. "They are saying she only has two to five days."

"Two to five days to what?" I asked.

But I already knew.

We called our other friend Melba and we made the decision to leave that night around midnight. Ten hours and we'd have our sweet Wendy in our arms again.

I tried not to cry as I watched Virgil wave good-bye as we drove away. Nothing felt like it was actually happening. Everything felt like a very bad dream.

We all agreed that I would start out driving, even though I probably have the worst eyesight of the bunch. Turns out that of the three of us, I felt the least uncomfortable driving at night—which was still pretty uncomfortable. I squinted and focused hard on the road in front of me, and that's how I did most of the driving.

Noreen sat in the passenger seat and used the GPS on her phone to navigate. Melba sat in the back. For the first few miles, none of us said a word. We just drove in silence, letting the reality of the situation sink in. But after a while, I got to talking. After all, talking is what I do best. Or at least, the most.

Not surprisingly, we talked about Wendy.

Wendy worked as a nurse, and I recounted a story another friend told me about Wendy's first day at a new hospital.

This other friend worked at the hospital, too, and she was in charge of taking Wendy around to show her how things worked. She was on a tight schedule, so she was hustling Wendy through the tour.

Then they came to a room where an elderly patient was sitting up in her bed. The woman's hospital gown was loose on her bony shoulders and her gray hair was bushy and wild. The woman stared off into space, at nothing. She wasn't in pain or distress or anything. She was just another lonely patient in another lonely hospital room, that's all.

The sight of her made Wendy stop in her tracks.

"Come on," my friend said, "we have to keep moving."

"One second," Wendy said in her sweet accent.

Wendy went to the little table beside the bed and opened the top drawer. She reached in and took out a hairbrush.

Then she sat on the bed beside the old woman and gently brushed her hair.

"There you go, dear," Wendy said, working through the tangles. "You're very beautiful, you know."

When she was done, she put the hairbrush back, leaned forward, and kissed the old woman on the forehead.

"Right, then," Wendy said to my friend. "Off we go."

My friend the nurse didn't say anything to Wendy at the time. But when she told the story to me, she said that Wendy's simple gesture was something she would never, ever forget.

"It changed me," she said. "It changed who I am as a nurse and as a person."

That was Wendy. Wendy changed the world by changing the people in *her* world.

We rolled up Route 44 on the way to Interstate 40, which would take us straight into Mississippi. I willed myself not to look at the dashboard clock or the odometer. I wanted the ten hours to feel like one or two. The traffic, not surprisingly, was light. For long stretches, we were the only car on the road, our headlights the only relief from the pitch black. We were a long way from Wendy, for sure, but at least we were heading in her direction now.

"We just have to see her," Melba said. "If we can just get to her, everything will be okay."

Noreen and I nodded. We were getting tiny little drips of information about Wendy's condition, and that just wasn't good enough. We couldn't talk to her. We couldn't ask her what was wrong or tell her she'd be okay. We needed more than what we had. We needed answers.

We needed to see our friend.

"If we can get to her, we can fix this," I said, agreeing with Melba. "We just need to get to her. I know God can heal her, I know it!"

I thought back to one of the last times I'd seen Wendy. It was the first Christmas after she'd moved away. When she told me Richard was taking a job in Southaven, Mississippi, I immediately broke down in tears and said, "No, you're not allowed to go." The day she left, I gave her a long hug but I didn't say good-bye. Instead I said, "See you later." I am terrible at good-byes, and this good-bye in particular was just about unbearable. But Wendy promised to call all the time and visit often, and sure enough, she was back at Christmas, and she came over to my house for dinner. It was like she had never left.

"Come on, take a picture of me and Crystal," Wendy said to Richard toward the end of the visit. Then she put her arm around me and pulled me close.

"No way, my hair is a mess," I said. "I look awful."

"Oh, come on now," Wendy said.

But I was insistent. I didn't want my picture taken. I was more worried about my appearance than commemorating our great day. So I pulled away from Wendy. Richard put his phone back in his pocket.

And now, driving up Route 44, I had a truly miserable thought.

Why didn't I just take the stupid picture?

A sign said "Oklahoma City." Another ten minutes and we'd be at Interstate 40. Steadily, we were eating up the miles.

Just another 492 to go.

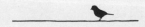

Wendy was one of the first people I shared my heaven story with. She is a devout Catholic who believes that heaven is real, and when her father died she had no doubt that's where he was. I was a little nervous about telling her my story, because I was nervous to tell my story to *anyone*. But nothing I said freaked Wendy out in the least. She just sat patiently and listened to me tell her everything.

"I am worried that people won't believe me," I said when I was done.

"Don't worry about the nonbelievers," Wendy said.

"I'm afraid they'll think I'm crazy. I'm afraid I will lose friends."

"Well, you won't lose this one," Wendy said. "I believe you."

The dashboard clock said 4:30 a.m. It was still dark outside, but the faintest light of morning was beginning to brighten the sky. In the passenger seat, Noreen had gamely stayed awake to keep me company, but now she was struggling not to doze off. We were low on gas and we needed a bathroom, so I pulled into a gas station.

Around that time, Noreen received a text on her phone. It was from another friend of ours, Sandra, who had been best friends with Wendy since they were young. Both became nurses and left England to work in Saudi Arabia during the war. They met and married men who took jobs at the same little military base back in the United States—the military base in my hometown. Sandra had set out for Mississippi with her family just a few hours ahead of us. She was texting to say that she was about an hour away from Southaven.

It was dawn now, and the sky was dreary and gray. We got back on the road and came upon some construction. For the first time, there was traffic. By then Melba was driving and I was in the backseat, fidgety because I couldn't wait to get to our friend. Every second we lost in traffic was a second we could have been comforting Wendy, telling her that everything was going to be okay. The sad truth was that we didn't *know* if she was going to be okay. And not knowing made it all so much worse.

We were still stuck in traffic when Noreen got another text. It was Sandra again. She had arrived and was sitting with Wendy.

"Where are you guys?" she wrote. "How far away?"

As Noreen read the text aloud, I felt my stomach sink. *That can't be good*, I thought.

Then we got a text from Wendy's husband, Richard. "Come straight to the house," he wrote, "and we'll go to the hospital together."

Twenty minutes later, he sent us another text.

This one said, "Go straight to the hospital."

That was followed by another text from Sandra.

"Where are you? How far away?"

Just then—at that very second—I felt Wendy's presence in the car with us, and I heard her say to me, "I love you, friend."

I looked at Noreen. I tried to speak but I couldn't. Finally, I said, "Wendy is gone."

Noreen was in tears. So was I. "Don't say that," she said. "Don't say that."

Melba kept driving. None of us said a word. The traffic let up, but we were still about twenty minutes away from the hospital. Noreen's cell phone rang.

Noreen quickly answered. As she listened, tears started flowing down her face. She threw her phone as hard as she could on the floor.

Through a terrible wail of pain, Noreen said, "She's gone."

Wendy's condition had been much worse than we knew. She had a massive clot on the left side of her brain. The doctors had told her husband that even with surgery, the damage already done would most likely leave Wendy in a vegetative state. This was something Wendy and Richard had talked about over the years. They each knew what the other wanted when it came to sustaining life. Richard made the heart-wrenching choice to follow Wendy's wishes and say no to the surgery. And he prayed Wendy would make it long enough to see her friends one last time.

But she didn't.

We finally arrived at the hospital and pulled into a parking spot. The three of us got out of the car and walked inside. We saw Richard and Robert in the lobby. I looked at Richard's tired, red eyes and I didn't know what to say. I had comforted many dying people, and I had said things that gave them solace. But now I was speechless. Instead I just hugged them both and cried.

Richard led us down a long hallway to Wendy's hospital room. I watched Richard and his son walk in front of us, and I noticed they had the exact same gait, which broke my heart. These men—these poor men—had just lost the love of their lives. When we got to the room, Richard turned to us and said, "Do you want me to take you in?"

I hesitated. I was barely holding it together, and I wasn't sure I wanted to go farther. But I knew I had to or else I'd regret it for the rest of my life.

Inside the room, I saw Wendy lying on the bed. Her head was tilted slightly to the right, and she looked like she was sleeping.

"We were with her when she passed," Richard said. "We already have had our good-byes with her, and we want to give you some time."

Noreen, Melba, and I stood around Wendy's bed. I leaned in and hugged Wendy and kissed her face.

"I'm so sorry," I said. "I'm so, so sorry. You are the greatest friend anyone could ever have, and I'm sorry I wasn't a better friend. I love you."

Melba bent over and kissed her, and then Noreen touched Wendy's arm and touched her hair and leaned in close.

"Wake up, Wendy," I heard her say. "Please, wake up."

We stayed with Wendy for about forty minutes, until someone came to take her away. I stroked her hair one last time and said, "I am forever changed by knowing you, friend. I'll meet you at the gate." Then we walked arm in arm in total silence out of the hospital and to the car, and drove to Richard's house. It was my first time in my friend's new home. I felt sick to my stomach that I hadn't come to visit her earlier.

When we are grieving and in shock, we sometimes find something to keep us busy—something to *do*. At Wendy's house, we immediately decided that we needed to start collecting photographs for Wendy's funeral. We went into her bedroom, which had a turquoise color scheme. Turquoise was her favorite color.

"Wendy, I really love what you've done here," I said aloud.

Just then Noreen came over and tapped me on the shoulder. "Crystal, you need to come and see this."

We walked to the back of the bedroom, where Wendy kept her desk. On the desk was a box, waiting to be mailed. A card was attached to the box, addressed: "To Micah and Willow." The note inside said, "I love you guys always."

Uncontrollably, I burst into tears. *Only Wendy*, I thought. *Only Wendy could send the twins presents while she's in heaven.*

We spent the rest of the day and night at Wendy's house, talking, crying, laughing, and reminiscing. At one point we went to her closet to pick out an outfit for her to wear for the funeral. Wendy was incredibly spontaneous and so fun loving, and we giggled as we remembered how she'd often spill food all over herself. In fact, she did it all the time. So when we looked through her closet and pulled out shirts and dresses, we saw that many of them had small food stains on them. That made us laugh, and it made us remember one of the best things about Wendy. She didn't care what people thought about her. All she cared about was sharing love with the people who mattered to her.

After a while we got hungry and went into the kitchen. Wendy enjoyed drinking Smirnoff wine coolers, and we found a few bottles and poured ourselves a drink. We also found some of Wendy's delicious English chocolate, and we had some of that, too. It's what Wendy would have wanted, we agreed as we laughed. She would have wanted us to drink and eat chocolate and laugh—just like we'd always done on our girls' nights together.

The next morning we went to the funeral home to help Richard make arrangements. There were lots and lots and lots of tears. Richard picked out a cemetery plot for Wendy, and he picked out another one for himself right next to hers. The funeral itself wouldn't happen for a few days, and I couldn't stay in Mississippi that long. Neither could Noreen or Melba. So we had to say our good-byes to Richard and Robert at the funeral home.

Rich hugged me tight. I could tell he was fighting hard to hold back tears.

"What am I going to do now?" he asked.

I had no answer for him.

"Crystal, what will I do without Wendy? She was my friend maker."

Before we left Mississippi, Noreen, Melba, and I went to lunch at the Texas Roadhouse—Wendy's favorite place. We all understood that Wendy had been the glue that held us together as a group, and we promised each other that no matter what, we wouldn't allow ourselves to drift apart. Suddenly, as I sat around the table eating barbecue with these wonderful women, I felt a strong urge to take a photo of the three of us. Not all that long ago, I would never have suggested taking a picture, and I probably would have protested if it had been someone else's idea. But not this time. Not anymore. This time, I didn't give a hoot what I looked like. We brought the waiter over and had him take the picture, another one for good measure, and several more after that.

Since then I have happily posed for *thousands* of photos with my friends.

We held a separate memorial service for Wendy in our hometown in Oklahoma. I was in charge of reserving a space for the service. The first man I spoke to at the funeral home told me it would cost $450 to set up the service. But when I came back later, another man asked me where the figure of $450 came from.

"One of your men told us that was the price," I said.

"Well, it's actually twice that amount," he said. "But I will honor what he told you."

I immediately thought of Wendy. One of the things she loved most of all was buying things on sale. She was a bargain hunter, and nothing pleased her more than a good bargain.

"Well, how about that, Wendy," I said to her on the way out of the funeral home. "I got your service at half price."

At the service we played one of my favorite songs—a song we believed truly summed up how we all felt about her. It was "For Good," from the musical *Wicked*.

"Because I knew you," the song goes, "I have been changed for good."

One of the hardest things I had to do was tell Micah and Willow about Wendy's passing. When I got back from Mississippi I sat with them and gave them the presents Wendy had for them on her desk. She bought a Sofia the First movie for Willow and a Ninja Turtles movie for Micah. The kids giggled in excitement over their gifts, and I felt myself start to lose it. But I quickly pulled it together, because I had to.

"Your aunt Wendy got sick and God needed her back in heaven," I told the twins. "She is going to wait for us in heaven, but she wanted you to have this one last present."

The twins looked sad and confused. Willow began to cry. A few days later, we dressed them up and took them with us to Wendy's memorial service. There was a slide show of photos of her, and then the pastor got up and started telling Wendy stories. All of a sudden I heard sniveling. I looked down, and I saw Willow was crying again. She was holding the memorial service program, which had a photo of Wendy on the first page, and she was looking at Wendy's smiling face and crying. I pulled her up onto my lap and wiped away her tears.

Then Willow reached up and wiped away mine.

In the days after Wendy's memorial service, when I finally had
time to be alone with my thoughts about losing her, I found that
I was having a hard time accepting what happened. Yes, I died
and went to heaven myself, and yes, I understood what a beautiful place it is. But even so, the one thing I couldn't get over about
Wendy's passing was how *unfair* it felt. I had never met anyone
as kind, good, loving, and godly as Wendy, and I was sure I never
would again. She had a beautiful life and loved her husband and
son more than anything, and yet God had taken her. Why?

I mean, the messed-up one was *me. I* was the sinner and the
skeptic. *I* was the one who doubted God and did bad things and
came up short as a friend to others. And yet God sent me back.
God took Wendy, and gave me more life. Why? How is that fair?

I had a long conversation with God, and I asked Him, *Why
Wendy?*

What got me through this difficult time—what eased the
pain and calmed my heart—was a knowledge that I didn't pos-
sess before I died.

The knowledge that I would soon see Wendy again, in heaven.

After Wendy passed, Richard arranged to have her finger-
print taken and used to make beautiful, sterling silver necklaces
for her friends and family. The inscription on the necklace read,
"A Touch of Wendy Forever." I desperately wanted to have one,
but they were expensive and we just didn't have the money at
the time. Melba and Noreen had to pass on the necklace, too. I
resigned myself to remembering Wendy in other ways.

Weeks later, Richard called me out of the blue.

"Do you remember those silver necklaces?" he asked.

"Sure I do," I said.

"Well, they made too many of them by mistake, and instead of throwing them away they said I could have them. Would you want one?"

I said yes, and Richard sent me a necklace. He also sent one to Melba and Noreen. We all knew the extra necklaces had not been a mistake.

They were Wendy's final gift to us from heaven.

CHAPTER TWENTY-THREE

Got Jesus?

NOT LONG AGO, SOMEONE SHOWED ME A PHOTO-graph of her friend's twins, William and Nicole. They are two years old and beautiful—from their radiant smiles I could just tell they are happy and well-loved. Looking at them, in all their innocence, is like looking at two perfect little angels. Every day, millions of parents send millions of photos of millions of beautiful children to their friends and loved ones, so you could say there wasn't anything unique about that photo of William and Nicole.

But to me there was.

The story of how the twins got to where they are today is not an ordinary story. It is not a pretty story; in fact it is very unpleasant. But it is also super important. The reason I decided to share it now is because when I heard it, it forever changed my way of seeing the world.

A friend of mine told me about a girl she knew named Liv. As soon as I heard even a tiny bit of Liv's story, I knew I had to meet her. I drove the three hours to where she lived and met her in the park on a bright summer afternoon. We sat on a bench beneath the trees, and I took my first good look at her. She had long dark-brown hair and piercing brown eyes, and she was a very beautiful girl. She had just turned twenty, but she seemed like someone much older. She started talking and told her story in a detached, matter-of-fact way. Almost as if she were talking about someone else. I knew this was a survival mechanism, because I had used it myself when I had to recall the painful and humiliating aspects of my own story.

For most of her life, Liv explained, she was stubborn and rebellious. She was raised by a single mom and had never known her father. She liked doing things her way. At sixteen, she gave birth to a child and raised him with her mom's help. At eighteen, she was introduced to the stage of a strip club and quickly fell into a world of smoke, dollars, and darkness. Her goal was to earn enough money to buy a car.

One night after she finished her set onstage, an older man approached her. He was handsome and well-dressed, and he flashed his money along with a dimpled smile. He told Liv that he owned a club about four hours away and that with her beauty and skill she could easily make somewhere near eight thousand dollars a week at his club. The idea of making all that money was too much for Liv to resist. She was smitten with the man and his promises to take care of her. Like so many lost girls, she longed for a man's love and protection. So she left her son with her mother and followed her dream of independence.

When they arrived in the new city, the man took Liv

straight to the apartment she would share with other dancers. Liv was excited to meet them. But as soon as she walked through the front door, she knew something was wrong. She didn't see the other dancers. All she saw were three other men. She turned to run, but the men grabbed her and dragged her to a back room.

Steadily and without expression, Liv told me how the four men raped and beat her repeatedly over the next two days. In between the attacks, they injected her with a syringe full of drugs. After a while, Liv began to welcome the drugs because they numbed her to the nightmare she was in.

After a few days Liv was finally allowed to meet the three other girls who lived in the apartment. One of them looked to be no more than thirteen years old. She was a runaway. None of the girls was allowed to have much contact with the others, and if they broke that rule they were beaten. Every day, men arrived and disappeared into the back room with one of the girls. Sometimes as many as forty men passed through the apartment in one day. Liv wanted to fight back, but then someone would put a gun to her head and the nightmare would continue.

Liv dreamed of escaping, but she was too terrified of her captors to do anything. One day a police officer entered the house. One of the girls ran up to the officer and told him what was happening. The officer turned to one of the captors and told him what the girl had just said. Then the officer walked out. Liv was forced to watch as the girl was severely beaten. From then on, none of the girls in the apartment dared reach out to anyone for help.

I later learned that is a common tactic used on girls who are trafficked for sex. A man poses as a police officer and rats out any girls who approach him. The beatings that follow ensure the girls stop trusting anyone.

A month into her ordeal, Liv began feeling extremely sick. One of the captors gave her a pregnancy test, and Liv cried when she saw the result—positive. The captor, posing as her boyfriend, took her to an abortion clinic. He warned Liv what would happen if she so much as breathed a word to anyone. But Liv knew this was her best chance at freedom. She watched as her captor spoke with a nurse, and then she asked another nurse if she could use the bathroom.

Liv's heart beat nearly out of her chest as she slipped out of her captor's eyesight, ran down a long hallway, and made a break for the back door of the clinic. She burst outside, into the bright light of the sun. *Run!* a voice in her head screamed. And run she did. She ran two blocks before ducking into a small convenience store. She saw a young man behind the counter, in a T-shirt that read, "Got Jesus?"

"Hide me," she begged him, her voice barely audible. "Please hide me."

The young man brought Liv around the counter and put her beneath it in a space just big enough for her to hide. He packed a few boxes around her and draped a cloth on top. He was still draping the cloth when Liv's captor came running through the door. He went up to the cashier and asked if he'd seen a young woman come in.

"No, sir," the boy said calmly.

The man looked up and down the aisles. Under the counter,

Liv pulled her knees up tight to her chest and tried to keep her legs from shaking. Finally the man left the store.

The young man offered to call the cops, but Liv begged him not to. Instead she borrowed his phone and called her mother. Her mother hadn't heard from Liv in a month and had no idea what had happened to her daughter. She drove three hours to pick Liv up and was horrified when she finally saw her. Liv's mom wrapped her coat around Liv and led her to the car. The young man in the "Got Jesus?" T-shirt watched them go.

That young man may never know his actions helped save more than one life that day. They also helped save the three tiny babies growing inside Liv.

A few months later Liv went into premature labor, and her tiny triplets were born—two boys and a girl. She looked at them with amazement and sadness through the glass of their incubators. Tragically, one of the baby boys didn't survive.

Arrangements were made for the surviving infants to be adopted. On the day that Liv left the hospital, she kissed her fingertips and placed them against the incubator glass and told the babies she loved them. Standing next to her with her arm around Liv's shoulders was the mother Liv had chosen for her babies through the adoption agency.

"I promise we'll give them a beautiful life," the woman said, wiping the tears from Liv's face. The woman's husband placed his hands on each woman's shoulder and prayed.

That was the last time Liv saw her children.

No matter how hard she tried to be stoic, Liv could not hide her unthinkable pain as she told me her story. I held her and prayed with her. I told her about a God that truly loves us. I tried to explain that God's greatest gift to each of us is the gift of free will, and that as much as He loves us, He will not take our free will from us. As a result, we are often hurt by the free will of others, and we wind up blaming God. Still, no matter what I said, I could not fix what was broken in Liv.

We hugged again and said good-bye, and that was the only time I spoke with Liv. I later learned that she left the state and soon slipped back into the darkness of drugs and prostitution. When I heard that, I felt like I'd let Liv slip through my fingers. In time I would learn there are thousands and thousands of girls just like Liv, and God is in an active war for each one of them.

I did some research into human trafficking, and the statistics are shocking. For one thing, it is the fastest-growing crime in our world today. Cases of human trafficking have been reported in all fifty states in the U.S. The average age of the victims is twelve years old.

Sadly, only 1 to 2 percent of victims are ever rescued.

Before I met and spoke with Liv, I had never thought of human trafficking as anything that touched my life. Now I know that was a naive and dangerous way to think. The factors that lead to nightmares like the one Liv found herself in actually take root within the walls of our "safe" lives. It begins in the homes of our friends, coworkers, neighbors, police officers, teachers, doctors, pastors, the people who sit beside us in church each Sunday—even our children.

Because the sad truth is that the growing rate of sex trafficking is directly affected by the demand for pornography. Every time someone views pornography in the privacy and safety of their own home, the vicious cycle of supply and demand that ensnares women like Liv continues. A 2003 study performed by Focus on the Family shows that nearly half of the men surveyed reported viewing pornography within a week of attending church. In fact, some 47 percent of the men admitted that pornography is a problem in their homes and marriages.

My prayer is that with more education, and with more brave women like Liv sharing their stories, our society might stop viewing this problem the way I once did—as not *my* problem.

And when I say this prayer, I also pray for Liv. Meeting her changed my life. The girls represented by all those statistics were no longer nameless or faceless to me. They were real, and they were someone's precious daughter.

They were my sisters.

CHAPTER TWENTY-FOUR

Destiny

S IT WITH THE HOMELESS AND WALK WITH YOUR sisters—that is what God told me in my dream. His message was clear, and yet, as I mentioned, I was confused. I knew beyond any doubt that God had spoken to my spirit about where He wanted me to focus my attention; I just wasn't sure how to go about it.

At the same time, I wasn't surprised God was steering my heart toward women in the sex industry. I wasn't surprised because I very nearly became trapped in that darkness myself. Meeting Liv just made me realize how close I'd come to meeting her same fate.

It happened a long time ago, when I was twenty-two. I was a divorced single mother with two kids, working two jobs but still falling short financially. I attended college classes three days a week and I worked behind the bar of a nightclub several nights a week. I was desperately trying to raise enough money to buy books for the upcoming semester when the owner of the club,

an Asian man people called "Inky," approached me. He told me
he was sending me over to tend bar at his other club, far outside
the city limits, for one night. I didn't want to go, because I knew
it was a strip club. Inky offered to pay me double my salary, and
reluctantly I agreed. I asked my coworkers at the nightclub not
to tell anyone where I was working that night, should anyone call
and ask. Especially if it was my mother.

But when my mom did call the nightclub, someone told her
where I was. She called me there and was practically hysterical.

"Get out of there now, Crystal," she demanded. "You are
worth more than this. You don't need money bad enough to sell
yourself!"

"Mom, I'm just bartending," I assured her. "It's only for one
night and it's going to pay for my college books. It's no big deal,
I promise."

Deep down, however, I knew it was. Yes, I was behind the bar,
but I could see full well what life was like for the young girls up
onstage. Some of them were older than me, some younger, but
most of them were right around my age. I imagined they were
like me in other ways, too—no husband, no money, maybe even
a couple of hungry kids.

What struck me most glaringly of all was how much money
the girls were walking away with. I watched as one of the dancers
who had just finished her set sat at the end of the bar and stacked
her earnings into a big pile. I could see how alluring the money
was, especially for someone like me—young, impressionable, and
broke.

"That could be you, Crystal," the club owner told me, pointing
to the stage. "You are beautiful and they would love you. See how
much money you'd make?"

I was a young girl who had longed to be loved her whole life, and the idea of all that money was tempting. But, as seductive as it was, it didn't take me long to politely decline. I quit the night-club and found a new job as a waitress at a country bar while I finished college.

Still, I've never forgotten that one night in the strip club. It opened my eyes to how easily girls get lured into the industry. They're exposed to the lifestyle, made to feel special, and shown dollar bills raining from the sky. That night, all I had to do was say one simple word and my life would have changed. All I had to do was say, "Yes."

Looking back, I realize what it was that kept me off the stage. Part of it was my own morals, but part of it was my mother. I simply couldn't bear the thought of trying to explain to her the path I'd chosen. I had my problems with my mother—Lord knows—but in the end she was the one who stopped me from making some pretty terrible choices in my life. It would have been so easy for me to say yes—*so easy*. But I didn't.

But I have to tell you, I was closer to it than I like to admit.

I often say I was one stiletto-heeled step away from getting up on that stage.

Many years and one trip to heaven later, God placed me on a different kind of stage—one where I was fortunate to speak to thousands of women about their worth and how much God loves them. And then I had a dream instructing me to sit with the homeless and walk with my sisters. God let me know it was time to go back into the strip clubs to share the reality of His love.

It took me many months to answer God's call. I guess I had to circle around the idea for a while. I'd found a way to minister to the homeless, but strip clubs were a different matter. I did a lot of research online and discovered a group in Texas that was devoted to ministering to women in strip clubs. I typed up an email expressing my interest in helping them in any way I could. Before long, I heard back from a woman named Heidi, inviting me to meet her for lunch. A few days later, I made the long drive over the Oklahoma border and into Texas to meet her at a coffee shop.

When I arrived, Heidi was already there. She was tall and thin and looked to be around my age, and she was wearing a big white T-shirt with purple leggings. Her long, curly blond hair was pulled off of her face with a headband, and she wore pretty feathered earrings. Her wrists were adorned with bracelets of tied strings. She looked like the perfect mix between a hippie and a rock star. We shook hands, and immediately I sensed she was warm, earthy, and deeply spiritual. I pegged her as an adventurous person, and I later learned that in her younger years, she couch-surfed around the world. There's actually a global community of couch-surfers who connect through an online network. They travel the world, crashing in people's homes and sleeping on their sofas for free. Couch-surfing isn't for everyone, but it fit Heidi perfectly. There was nothing shy or hesitant about her.

Heidi had never married, but she was a foster mother caring for the young daughter of one of the dancers she'd befriended.

That is just the kind of person Heidi is.

"So what's your story?" she asked right off the bat. "Why do you want to do this?"

By way of answering, I probably said about a million words to explain my reasons, but what it boiled down to was this: I was that girl, the one full of secrets and shame, who felt worthless. Yet God chose to save me. He saved me from a life of destruction and anguish. God changed my life and He changed me forever. And now He had called me back into the darkness for my sisters.

Heidi eyed me up and down as I finished my story and asked her to please let me join her mission. Finally she smiled, reached into her bag, and pulled out some papers. "You'll need to sign these," she explained. Then, without even telling me I'd been accepted, she began explaining the rules of going into the clubs.

"Keep your eyes on their eyes," she said. "Their bodies are for sale. They're degraded and disrespected every day. So keep your eyes on their eyes."

We sat there drinking coffee and sharing stories. Heidi spoke about the triumphs and heartbreak that came with her line of work. I laughed and I cried and we prayed together.

When I signed the papers, Heidi yelled out, "Welcome, sista!"

According to several studies, there are more women caught up in the sex industry today than at any other time in history. There are also more strip clubs in the United States than in any other country. The larger and broader problem of human trafficking affects many millions of women each year. By some estimates, there are 20 to 30 million people who are enslaved in some way in the world today.

Working in a strip club is one of the ways women get pulled into this dark and often deadly underground world.

What's more, statistics show that roughly 66 to 90 percent of women working in the adult entertainment clubs were sexually

abused before the age of eighteen. These women are my sisters—
the very women God was steering me toward.

But first, God directed me to Heidi. The goals of her ministry
are simple and powerful. In her words, the ministry aims to help
women in strip clubs "experience the breaking of chains and healing of wounds through a personal relationship with Jesus Christ."
To go into the darkness and bear witness to the truth "that there
is a God Who loves these women beyond measure."

Twice a month, Heidi and her small team venture into the
clubs and hand the dancers small bags filled with beautifully
wrapped gifts such as candles, scarves, homemade cookies,
gourmet treats, or a bottle of perfume—something different
each month. Tucked inside the gift bags are handwritten notes
with messages of love and affirmation for the women, as well as
a card with the phone number of Heidi's ministry. There isn't
any preaching or lecturing or passing out of Bibles—just an
offer to talk and, more important, to listen. As Heidi often says,
her ministry isn't results driven—it's *relationship* driven. And
when a woman is ready to leave the sex industry, Heidi helps
find counseling and services that she hopes will assist these ladies "on the journey to becoming the women God created them
to be."

A month after I met Heidi in the coffee shop, Virgil drove
me the three hours back to Texas. I was supposed to meet Heidi
and her team at a little coffee shop, where we'd get ready to go to
the strip clubs. Virgil and I pulled up in front of the place around
7:00 p.m. On the street outside the shop, all sorts of people were
hanging around. Some appeared to be homeless or transient. A
few children ran on the sidewalk, playing around the clouds of
cigarette smoke.

"Uh, you know this isn't the greatest neighborhood," Virgil said in his calm, understated way.

Almost involuntarily, I pushed my purse up under my seat and I locked the car doors.

"Let's just sit here awhile," I said.

After a few minutes I noticed a small white van pull up beside us. It had the name of a church on the side. The door opened, and a tiny woman popped out. She looked like she was five foot two and maybe ninety pounds. I watched as she walked up to all the people standing outside the coffee shop.

And I watched as, one by one, she hugged them all.

Instantly my fears subsided. I clearly still had a lot to learn about this world.

"Okay," I said to Virgil, "here we go." Virgil gave me a kiss, wished me luck, and told me he'd be back to pick me up as soon as I was done.

In the coffee shop, I found a group of four women at a wobbly table in the back. Two of the ladies looked to be about my age, while two appeared much younger. We all looked at each other and nodded but didn't say much. I felt out of place and unsure of myself, so I stayed quiet. Suddenly I heard a bit of a commotion. I turned to see a woman bounding up to our table. It was Heidi.

I got up to shake her hand. Instead she wrapped her arms around me and squeezed.

"Everybody, this is our new sister, Crystal!" Heidi loudly announced. "Everybody say hi!"

The ladies cheerily greeted me, and we all sat down. A few more women walked in and joined us.

"Crystal has an awesome testimony," Heidi went on. "Go ahead, tell 'em."

I shared my story, but truthfully, I was far more interested in learning about these women. What were *their* stories? How had God led them to get involved with this ministry? Was it the same way He had led me?

"Okay, let's start," Heidi said when I was finished. "Everyone go around and tell us the worst thing that happened to you this week."

No one batted an eye. One girl said she didn't know if she could pay her rent. Another said she was fighting for her marriage. One woman shared how her son had broken his ankle in a soccer tournament. Another, who left the clubs five years ago, said a friend of hers she'd danced with at the strip club had died from a drug overdose. Over cups of coffee, and right in front of me—a total stranger—these women shared the darkest parts of themselves in such a real and sincere way. I leaned over to Heidi.

"This gets pretty deep," I said.

"Honey, we haven't even started."

After a short devotional and some prayers, it was time to go.

"Okay, ladies," Heidi yelled out. "Y'all ready to rock and roll!?!"

I felt my stomach tie up into knots again, but still I hollered that I was ready. All of us did. The energy in this group was amazing. We went outside and piled into the van.

"So the church lets you use their van?" I asked Heidi.

"What the church doesn't know won't hurt them," she said with a wink. I had no idea if she was kidding or not.

The tiny woman I saw get out of the van when I first arrived with Virgil—whom I learned was named Abby—climbed in behind the wheel, and we started driving. We left at sundown, right around 8:00 p.m. Within a few minutes, the van had pulled over and stopped outside the first club.

I felt a little bit of relief. The club wasn't that seedy; in fact it looked kind of classy. The bouncer outside was nicely dressed and the men going in were, too. Heidi, in the passenger seat, turned to face us sitting in the back.

"Okay, who wants to go in first?" she asked.

I sat on my hands and didn't say a word.

"Crystal, thanks for volunteering!" Heidi said.

She handed me several gift bags and I eased my way out of the van. Heidi typically sent a team of four women into each club, while the rest of the group stayed in the van and prayed. We went in two at a time, and Laura, one of the younger women, came with me. Laura was maybe twenty years old, but when I looked at her, she didn't appear scared at all. I momentarily felt ashamed for being so fearful. Heidi came out and handed me another bag filled with gourmet treats.

"That's for the bouncer, the door guy, and bartenders," she said.

I'd wondered how it was that Heidi and her volunteers could so easily walk in and out of the clubs. After all, they weren't exactly good for business. To my surprise, Heidi told me her goal wasn't getting the girls out of the clubs. "Our goal," she said, "is to love our sisters right where they are. No expectations or agendas. Now, if they choose to leave, then of course we walk with them through that journey, too. I asked Heidi if the club owners were afraid of losing their girls. Her answer surprised me again.

"They don't care," she said. "If they lose one girl, there's ten others lined up behind them waiting for the job."

The club owners tolerated Heidi's team because, as far as they were concerned, Heidi's team *made no difference.*

It was truly a sad thought.

Laura and I walked up to the bouncer, carrying our many bags. The bouncer greeted Laura like an old friend. He was friendly and polite as he accepted his bag of treats with a gracious thank-you. Then he waved us on inside.

We moved into the club and through a dark hallway. A woman behind a desk was checking IDs and taking in the cover charge. As soon as she saw Laura, she got up and came over.

"How are you, sweetheart?" the woman asked.

"I'm great, how are you?"

The woman said one of her friends had been shot the day before, and asked Laura to pray for her. Laura reached over the counter and hugged the woman and began whispering prayers in her ear.

A middle-aged man was standing beside them, waiting to pay to go in. He looked over at me, and I quickly looked away. I'm sure he was confused and perhaps even annoyed. After all, he didn't come to a strip club to watch people *pray.* After a minute or so of waiting, he grew impatient and asked the woman if he could pay and go in. She held up one finger.

"Hold on," she said. "In a minute."

She finished her conversation with Laura, gave her a hug, and motioned us inside.

"Y'all are good, go on in," she said.

The place was packed with men of all ages. Loud rock music was blaring from the speakers. On the big stage, several young women danced halfheartedly wearing nothing or next to nothing. I remembered the rule—look at their eyes—and I tried to do just that. But it was hard. I struggled to keep my eyes from darting everywhere in the club—at the men, at the girls, everywhere. So much was going on. I regained my focus and stared at the back of Laura's head as she led me through the club. One of the prayers we said earlier at the coffee shop was a prayer not to let anything we saw at the clubs seep into our minds. Heidi understood that the images of men buying women were, once seen, impossible to unsee. We had to be careful to focus on what mattered.

There was another important rule Heidi had explained to me earlier—we were never to approach the dancers on the floor of the club. We were only to go up to them in the back, in their dressing rooms. We were supposed to respect the women and the place where they worked, no matter how we may have felt about it personally. One of the reasons the club owners let Heidi keep coming back was because her team was so courteous and considerate. We weren't there to make a scene or to make anyone uncomfortable. We were there to share love with the dancers, and that was all. With that in mind, Laura and I quickly made our way through the club and headed to the back.

But before we got there, one of the dancers stopped us.

She was young and beautiful, with dark skin and a wide smile. Three men, each with several bills in their hands, were seated around her. She didn't step away from them; she just leaned toward us, catching our arms before we could go.

"Hey, what do you guys have there?" she asked.

"We have gifts," I said.

"Oh yeah?" She reached into her garter belt to pull out a small clump of bills. "What are you selling tonight?"

"We're not selling anything," Laura said. "These are free."

"Free?" She laughed. "Why are they free?"

"Because we love you," Laura said.

The girl tucked her money back in her garter belt.

"Oh," she said. "Are you girls with a church or something?"

"We're not with any church," Laura said. "We just love God and we come together for this because we love our sisters. We love *you*."

The dancer looked us over. The three men waited with their money in their hands. I tried not to look at them, but I couldn't help it. They looked somewhere between angry and embarrassed. I forced myself to look straight at the dancer, in her eyes.

"My name is Destiny," she said finally.

Another rule was that we weren't supposed to ask the girls for their real names. Destiny, Starlight, Roxie, Snow White—whatever name they gave us, that is what we called them. Having a girl tell you her real name was a rare show of trust and openness, and when it happened, Heidi and her team would treat it as cause for celebration. It was one of the few ways they could tell they were getting through. But like anything else precious, it couldn't be asked for. It had to be earned.

"Hi, Destiny," I said. "I'm Crystal."

"Is there anything we can be praying about for you?" Laura asked.

"Oh, no, I'm good," Destiny said. "You don't need to pray for me." She took another step toward us and said, "You know, I used to go to church all the time when I was little. I used to pray all the time."

"Okay," said Laura. "Will you pray for me?"

"Oh, sure, girl, yeah, yeah. I will pray for you."

I could feel the three men alternately staring and looking

away. I can only imagine what was going through their heads. Destiny took our hands and we bowed our heads.

"Here I go," she said.

Then—silence. Nothing.

"Hold on, just give me a sec," Destiny said. "Haven't done this in a while."

And then it happened.

"Father," she began, "bless Your child Laura and Your child Crystal. Please hear our prayer . . ."

I didn't hear anything after that. The music was blaring, but that wasn't why. It was that she began her prayer with "Father." She called Him Father. I was stunned. Here I was in the middle of a strip club, a place dark with sin and shame, and a girl named Destiny was calling out to her Father. *It took my breath away.* She hadn't prayed in who knows how long, but she hadn't forgotten Who she prayed to. When she finished, she gave us each a big hug. Laura handed her a bag, and we began to shuffle toward the back. But before we could go, Destiny stopped us again.

"By the way," she said, "my real name is Shannon."

And then she went back to dancing.

We made our way to the fairly clean dressing rooms and found eight women getting ready for their sets.

Most were very young, but some were about my age. They all sat around fussing with their makeup and slipping in and out of clothes. When we walked in, most of them didn't even notice. They were used to being stared at and approached. A couple more people bothering them while they were changing wasn't a big deal.

Laura and I went around the room passing out gifts and asking the women how they were doing. Many of them recognized Laura and were happy to see her. The women oohed and aahed as they opened their presents, and we stayed for a while, chatting and laughing. I was surprised by how easy and friendly the whole experience was. It made me reflect on Heidi's mission—to love the women right where they were. The gifts were unconditional. There was no sales pitch. All we wanted was for the girls to know they were loved and they weren't alone.

"We better get going," Laura said. "We love you guys. We'll see you next month. If you need anything, don't forget to call us."

Back in the van, Heidi asked how it went.

"One of the girls told us her real name," Laura said.

"Well, glory to God!" Heidi yelled out as the other girls loudly cheered.

I took my seat and smiled to myself.

"Okay then," Heidi said, "let's keep going!"

Abby steered us to the next club. I figured I wouldn't go into this one, since I had just gone in the first one. When we pulled up to the club, I immediately noticed it wasn't nearly as nice as the first one. I was more than happy to stay behind and pray in the van.

"Crystal, you're up again!" Heidi announced.

This time it was Heidi who came in with me and two other girls. The bouncer recognized her right away and ushered us in. Heidi walked quickly and purposefully, and I had to hustle to keep up. We walked straight into the club, past the stage, and to the dressing rooms. All of a sudden I heard the music stop. After a moment a new song came on. It was the old power ballad "Sister Christian" by the eighties rock band Night Ranger. The lyrics blared loudly through the club.

> *Sister Christian, oh, the time has come*
> *And you know that you're the only one*
> *To say, okay*

Heidi pumped her fist in the air and let out a whoop.

"*Rock on!*" she yelled as she passed the DJ booth.

"He always plays that when we come in," she yelled back to me.

I laughed out loud. Here I was—wife, schoolteacher, mother of four—getting serenaded by the DJ in a strip club. It was funny, but it was also, in a weird way, beautiful.

Heidi and I spent fifteen minutes in the dressing room, chatting with the women and handing out gift bags. Then it was back to the van and on to the next club. In all, we drove to sixteen clubs that night. Not every club manager was happy to see us. One female manager stopped us on our way in and took Heidi's arm in hers and walked us all straight back out of the club. She was reasonably polite about it, and Heidi didn't seem upset. She hugged the manager and told her we would see her next month.

"That was the farthest we've ever made it into that club," she said. "We'll make it all the way in someday."

After a while, the strip clubs began to blend together. Most were slightly less grungy than I'd expected, but a few were even sleazier than I would have dared imagine. One, in particular, stood out.

We drove up to this club at around 2:00 a.m. Outside, seven or eight men stood around, smoking and talking. I didn't know exactly where we were, but it was easy to see we were in the very worst part of town. The most *dangerous* part of town. At this hour of the night, the street seemed all but deserted, save for the handful of men outside the strip club. If I had to guess, I'd say some of the men were part of a gang. Whoever they were, they didn't look the least bit friendly or welcoming. I felt my muscles seize up. Whatever strength and confidence I'd stored up earlier that night just went away. Instead, I felt a powerful urge to be anywhere else but there. *Run away,* a voice inside me said. *You're not safe here.*

But I knew I couldn't run away.

Of course Heidi picked me to go into this club. And she picked tiny Abby to pair up with me and go in. We grabbed the gift bags and headed toward the impossibly beefy bouncer.

"Hey, church ladies," he yelled out. "Come here."

Abby handed the bouncer a bag of gourmet treats.

"What you got for me tonight?" he asked. "I hope it ain't fattening, you know I got to watch my weight." Then he burst out laughing.

I was hoping something would happen that stopped us from going inside the club. But the bouncer just motioned us inside. We opened the thick metal door and stepped into the deep darkness. There was nothing elegant or classy about the club at all. This club was more like a dungeon. The paint on the walls was peeling and some parts of the room were falling apart. The air was dense with smoke, and the red neon lights gave the place a sinister glow. The men, too, weren't like the men I'd seen in the other clubs. These men weren't wearing suits and ties. When they turned to look at us, all I could feel coming from them was menace and hate.

"Stay right behind me," tiny Abby said.

"No," I said, "you should get behind me. None of these guys are going to be interested in me. You'll be safe behind me." I was making a joke, but it was just a nervous joke. The truth was, I was scared to death. I was truly, genuinely concerned for my safety. I found myself praying out loud for God's protection. I had to suppress a powerful urge just to turn around and run like crazy back to the van.

Back to my life.

Only later would I realize—"Crystal, this *is* your life now."

Suddenly there was a commotion in the club. People were dashing around and chairs were getting knocked over. Some of the dancers were rushing to the front door.

"I'm getting out of here," one of them said.

Something was going down.

Still, Abby held her ground. One of the dancers came over to talk to us, but before long more girls were gathering their things and leaving. It became clear we weren't safe anymore. Abby and I put the bags down near the dressing room as the girls packed their bags. One of the dancers looked at me and said, "Girl, y'all follow me. It's time for us all to get out of here." She took Abby's hand and led us out of the club and into the darkness of the night. When we got to the street, I walked so quickly to the van I nearly tripped. My face was white with fear.

Back in the safety of the van, I looked at Abby. Like me, she was breathing kind of hard. She looked over and smiled.

"My spirit was telling me to get the heck out of there," she said.

"Mine too!" I panted.

"You know," Abby said, "it's okay to be scared."

I nodded, happy she'd said that.

I never found out what the commotion was all about, but not much later police shut the club down after someone was shot inside.

Sometime in the middle of the night—between the twelfth and thirteenth strip clubs—we stopped at a place the girls called Jesus Tacos. It was a simple little Mexican place, but the tacos were delicious, and we sat around and talked about our lives and laughed. It was one of the best meals I ever had.

I found out more about Heidi's ministry. I learned that several of her volunteers were former dancers themselves. One of them had been a dancer in her younger days, but then had gotten too old to dance. Instead she worked the bar in a strip club, same as I once had. One day Heidi came into her club and told her how much she was loved. The woman put down the drink she was making and walked out of the club with Heidi. The next time she entered that club, it was with a gift bag in her hand.

I discovered that Heidi handed out gift bags to about three hundred women every month. She worked on the mission full-time, and her salary was exactly zero dollars. Everything that went into the gift bags was donated. I had no idea how Heidi managed to keep the whole operation afloat. I know how hard it was for me to juggle the few bills I pay every month and tend to my four kids—I couldn't image how Heidi juggled her three hundred women, plus the young girl she was fostering. I asked her point-blank how she could possibly live that way.

"Faith," is all she said.

When we were done eating, we climbed back into the van and

headed to the next club. I gathered up some gift bags and got ready to go in. Heidi stopped me and handed me a small book. It was my book. The book that told the story of my life and the darkness God rescued me from.

"See if you can find a good place for this in there somewhere," she said with a wink.

I was startled by the request. I took the book and stuffed it up under my shirt. I didn't want anyone to see me carrying it.

A tall, young volunteer named Alicia went into the club with me. We walked past the stage and made our way to the back. This club was darker than the others, and more run-down—not the worst one, but awfully close. We walked up the stairs to the dressing rooms, which were basically a series of stalls separated by dirty curtains. Some of the curtains were open, and I could see women getting ready to dance, sitting together, and talking. Some of the girls recognized Alicia and we began passing out gift bags.

Then something drew me to the very last stall in the back of the room. A nudge pulled me toward it. I didn't know what I would find there, but I knew it was the place I needed to be. I knew that whatever was in that stall was the reason God had brought me out that night. I gathered up my courage and walked slowly to the end of the long row of stalls. Stopping at the last one, I saw that the curtain was closed. I tried to peer through, but I couldn't see anything. I didn't want to disturb whoever was in there, but I knew I couldn't just turn around and walk away, either. I said a silent prayer and asked God for courage. Hesitantly, I said, "Hello?" and pulled back the curtain a tiny bit, trying to look through.

The stall was empty. There was a green duffel bag on the floor, with a red bra and some other lingerie sticking out. There was a little shelf on the wall, and on that shelf were three small, framed photos.

The photos were of children.

Two tiny, adorable kids. Happy, smiling kids. Just like the photographs I have at home. But on the shelf next to the photos was a bottle of Crown Royal whisky.

The bottle was empty and lying on its side.

I stood in the stall and held my breath and looked around. In an instant, I knew just who this woman was. I felt the intense cord of love that bonded me to her as a fellow human being. A fellow *child of God*. My *sister*. I reached under my shirt, pulled out my book, and laid it on the shelf between the photos of the smiling kids and the bottle of Crown.

"You are crowned in the royalty of God," I said.

I had no idea if the woman would pick it up and read it; maybe she'd just throw it in the trash. But if she *did* open it, if she was *brave* enough to open it, I knew there was a chance that she would feel God's love rise up from its pages and embrace her just as strongly and as fiercely as His love had embraced me.

I turned to leave, but before I did I took one last look at the dancer's dingy stall. The rug was stained and fraying. There were empty lipstick tubes and other junk on the floor. The smell of smoke and beer filled the stale air. The room was so dark, dirty, and dreary it made me want to cry.

I looked at the book and I thought:

This is the most beautiful place I've ever shared my story.

CHAPTER TWENTY-FIVE

The Starfish

I WAS JUST ABOUT TO GET ONSTAGE AND SPEAK AT a women's conference in New Mexico when I got a text message from Heidi. It was simple and to the point.

"T still wants to have an abortion. Keep praying."

"T" was how Heidi referred to one of the dancers she'd met through her strip club mission. Heidi was always careful to protect the privacy of the women she became friends with in the clubs, so she used only their initials in texts and emails. I had learned from the girls in the clubs that prostitution was common, and while most of them were against it, T had unfortunately stopped dancing and started selling herself on the streets. Now she was pregnant, and Heidi was right there, walking with her through the journey and praying.

By then I'd been training under Heidi long enough to understand why her ministry worked. She knew she couldn't approach the girls by yelling "God loves you!" Heidi knew exactly what was successful—establishing a true and meaningful relationship with the people she was ministering to. I understood that really well. I often say it was relationship and not religion that saved me, and Heidi's approach spoke right to my heart.

"It's not just ministry," Heidi says. "It's doing life together and it's beautiful and messy and amazing. So buckle up, buttercup!"

With someone like T and some of our other sisters in the clubs, one false move could wipe out years of trust and friendship. It was a delicate dance and it kind of reminded me of fishing. If you throw a rock in the water, all the fish will scatter. Instead, Heidi worked slowly and built trust with the girls. In fishing, you have to stand quietly in the water so that the fish get so comfortable with your presence, they forget you are even there. Eventually a fish will get hungry enough to bite what you are offering. For me, watching how Heidi worked with these women brought the words of the Lord to life. Our Savior told His disciples in Matthew 4:19, "Follow Me and I will make you fishers of men" (ESV). For the first time, I truly understood that Scripture.

More than anything, Heidi wanted T's child to be born, because she knew the value of that unborn baby, and that all life was precious. But she also understood the decision was not hers to make. All she could do for T was walk beside her and continue to exemplify the love of the Lord through her deeds. And she could pray.

That's why she texted me with her request. T's mind seemed to be made up, and the hours were ticking by. Heidi needed as many prayers as she could get.

I got up onstage at the women's conference and faced the three hundred women assembled in the audience. At the podium, I had my notes in my hands. My head told me I was supposed to go ahead and give my speech—the same speech I had given hundreds of times. But my heart was telling me something else.

Slowly, I put the speech notes down. I looked out at the crowd of women, and I began to tell a different story altogether.

"Today, before this conference is over, three thousand babies will be aborted," I said. "Not this week, or this month. Today. And those will be added to the almost fifty-five million that have taken place in my lifetime. Fifty-five *million* babies, and one of them was mine."

I told the women about the moment I walked through the doors of an abortion clinic as a frightened teenager, and about how I walked out completely broken. I shared how seventeen years later, God led me out of the shame and into His redemptive arms.

"The world gives us statistics, but these babies are not statistics," I said. "My child was not a statistic. He was my baby and his life mattered."

Then I told them about T. I told them how T was on the verge of making the same life-altering decision I'd made all those years ago. I urged the women to keep T and her precious baby in their prayers that day, and I picked up my notes and got ready to go on with my intended speech.

But then I noticed one woman rise from her seat and begin to pray out loud. I watched as other women followed her lead and stood to outstretch their hands to the heavens and pray for this little baby in T's belly. I watched an elderly woman carefully kneel before her chair and began to pray and plead for the child's life. Statistics say one out of every three women in this country are affected by abortion, and by that measure I knew many women in that room understood firsthand the lifetime of pain, shame, and guilt an abortion brings. And yet there we all were, joined together in prayer for two precious lives—T and her unborn baby.

I was witnessing nothing less than women becoming warriors.

My own experience with abortion, and the deep, deep shame I carried with me for so long, fueled my prayers for T. And the roomful of women who were praying with me—they filled me with hope and strength.

Later that evening, as I was preparing to go back up onstage and say a final good-bye to the women, I got another text message from Heidi.

"T saw the baby on ultrasound. There will be no abortion."

Turning away from someone in their time of greatest darkness is not loving. It cannot be what God wants us to do. Instead we must turn *toward* them and walk with them into the dark. That is what Heidi does each and every day—she walks beside these women, on the streets, in the clubs, everywhere. To see how much she loves people has taught me so, so much. Heidi does not see skin color. She does not see class. She does not see religion. When she looks at the faces of these women, she does not see what the world sees. She looks past the scars of addiction and the physical toll their burdens take on their faces. *All she sees is a beautiful, perfect daughter of God.* There isn't one ounce of judgment. There is only love—love for her fellow humans, and love for God.

And in the face of impossible odds, there is unending compassion.

Heidi makes me think of a beautiful old story many of us know—the story of the starfish on the beach. A young man is walking along the ocean and sees thousands of starfish washed ashore. He picks one up and throws it back in the water. Then he picks up another one and throws it back, too. He does this for starfish after starfish, even as more and more of them wash ashore. Another man comes along and says, "Why are you doing that? You can't possibly save all of them."

The young man picks up a starfish, throws it in the ocean, and says, "Maybe not, but I can help save this one."

God wants us to be throwers of starfish.

I often think back to the moment in heaven when God showed me that sweet little three-year-old girl dancing and laughing in His light. When I looked at her, I saw her as perfect and pure, and I was unable to contain the love I felt for her. God was showing me what I looked like *through His eyes*. I wasn't the wretched, broken, and unforgivable sinner I believed myself to be. I was His daughter, worthy of His love, and worthy of my own.

Then I came back to earth, and a few years later I met Heidi, and she showed me the same beautiful generosity of spirit, the same expansive love for all God's children. Except now I wasn't seeing it in heaven. I was seeing it in dark strip clubs and dangerous back alleys.

I was seeing God's love in action, right here on earth.

A few months after I got back from the women's conference, I was handing out gifts to my sisters in the clubs with my friend Katie when we got a phone call from Heidi.

"Do you guys have any cookies left?" she asked Katie.

Katie told her that we did.

"Great, head over to T's place and bring them to her," Heidi said. "Make sure Crystal goes in with you."

I knew Heidi had been staying in close touch with T throughout the pregnancy. She wasn't just giving her moral support—she was driving over in the middle of the night to drop off food, bringing her Sprite to help with her nausea, and handwriting love notes on a coffee cup to make T smile. She went with her on visits to the doctor. Even on this night when she was busy helping someone else, Heidi wanted to make sure T got some homemade cookies. I was happy to go, because I'd been following T's story and continuing to pray over her. I hadn't met her, but I truly felt like I knew her.

We pulled into the parking lot of a motel. It looked like one of those cheap motels that rent rooms by the hour. It was one in the morning when we got there, and the place was deserted. Katie and I gathered up the cookies and walked to T's room on the ground floor. Gently, I knocked on the door.

Immediately I heard shuffling through the door. A full minute went by, and still the shuffling continued. I knocked again, and we waited another three minutes or so before, finally, the scuffed-up motel door opened an inch or two.

I saw a tall woman in a curly red wig. Her eyes seemed a bit glazed over, and she didn't appear to be 100 percent there. I smiled as my eyes fell to her big, protruding belly, which pushed her T-shirt out. I looked back up in her eyes and said, "It's nice to meet you, T. I'm Crystal, a friend of Heidi's."

T looked at us hard and squinted, perhaps trying to figure out if she knew us. Then she smiled and called out to someone over her shoulder.

"See, I told you it wasn't the police," she said. "It's the dang church ladies."

I laughed. Yes, we *were* the dang church ladies. I looked past T, into the dark room. There were two other girls there who looked to be in their early twenties. It was hard to see their faces, but even so I noticed a blank and distant look in their eyes. It was something I'd seen over and over again in the clubs. So many of the girls end up on drugs or abusing alcohol to escape or cope, and then it becomes an endless cycle. In order to work, they need the drugs, and in order to get the drugs, they need to work.

T stood in the doorway, brushing her face to keep a wayward curl from her wig out of her eyes. Casually, she lit up a cigarette. The "old" me would have been judgmental about what she was doing, but in that moment, I felt no judgment. I only felt love and compassion. My only thought was, *What has been done to you?*

Don't get me wrong, it's not that I approved of what she was doing. It was that I could see beyond it. I also understood that if I'd said something critical to her at that point—without the context of a meaningful relationship with her—T most likely would have slammed the door in our faces. We might have lost the beautiful relationship God was building between her and Heidi.

I realized that when you choose to walk with people into their darkness, it isn't always pretty and it can get very messy.

"We had some extra cookies," I said to T. "I know that when I was pregnant that's all I wanted."

"All right!" T said excitedly, taking three bags of cookies and tossing two of them back to the other girls. She bit into a chocolate chip cookie and kept talking to us in the doorway. There was so much I wanted to tell her, and so much I held back. But I couldn't stop myself from saying how proud I was of her for choosing life.

"I know what that decision is like," I said, "and I know that when I didn't choose life for my own baby, it ended up destroying me."

"Yeah," T said with a nod. "I know that feeling, too."

A conversation slowly opened up. I shared some of the lowlights of my life—the sexual abuse, the early pregnancies, the abortion, the shame, and the self-hatred. I shared my doubts about God and how I hadn't known how to accept His love or my own.

"Girl," T said when I was done, "you're telling the story of my whole life."

"Do you know what you're having?" I asked her.

"A boy," she said. "He's kicking right now. Do you want to feel him?"

I reached over and gently laid my hand on T's belly. I felt her child's swift, hard kick, and in the same moment I felt a burst of joy in my heart. This was a child who was supposed to die, and yet I was feeling him move around in her belly. I was feeling life where death had been scheduled. A life saved because of people like Heidi, who dare to love the Lord and follow Him into the brothels, drug dens, and strip clubs. People who dare to love those whom others shun and cast away.

"What are you going to name him?" I asked T, my hand still on her stomach.

All of a sudden her demeanor changed, and the smile vanished from her face.

"He ain't got a name," she said. "I'm giving him away."

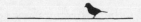

Heidi had been praying for T to give her child a name, so T could feel bonded to the precious child she chose to give life to, but I think T was struggling with that idea. She knew she was giving her baby up for adoption, and I'm sure she felt hesitant to bond with the child. In a perfect world, T would have accepted all of the help Heidi was ready to give her. She would have let Heidi give her a fresh start, away from the motels and the men who paid for her body. Perhaps even a path to becoming the mother her baby needed. But Heidi understood that for T to even begin to think of accepting that kind of help, she would first have to want the baby kicking inside of her. Heidi prayed every day for God to whisper this child's name to T.

I understood Heidi's thinking about as well as anyone could. I understood it, because for seventeen long years my own baby didn't have a name.

After my abortion, I didn't talk about what happened with anyone. All the guilt and shame I felt was mine and mine alone. I would keep the truth of my child a secret until the day I died. Every year, on the anniversary of my abortion, I locked myself away and cried for hours. But on the outside, I went about my life as if my baby had never existed. And if a baby doesn't exist, then he doesn't need a name.

It was only after I died and experienced the redemptive love of God that I realized God loved me in spite of what I'd done. For the first time in seventeen years, I was able to begin to talk about my abortion and the child I still grieved for.

Almost a year after I went to heaven, I sat down to do one of the hardest things I've ever had to do—tell my family about my unborn child. Up until then, Virgil was one of only a few people who knew about my abortion. I'd shared it with him before we got married, and Virgil chose to love me anyway.

Telling my parents was another story, but I was ready after experiencing heaven. To my surprise, they were both overwhelmingly supportive and understanding. My mom told me she was sorry I'd felt like I couldn't go to her and instead went through something like that alone. My father told me that it would never change his opinion of me or his love for me. I told my oldest children, Payne and Sabyre, separately, and that was really hard. Payne was hurt and angry, and Sabyre didn't say much at all. I allowed them to have their own feelings about it, and I said they could ask me any questions they wanted. Eventually we were able to talk about the sibling they never knew they had.

It was through these conversations that I saw how an abortion affects an entire family—even entire generations. My parents grieved for a grandchild they couldn't save, and my children grieved for a brother they would never know.

Two years after I died, the anniversary of my abortion approached. One night while I was praying, God led me to give my child a name as a way to celebrate his life. I gathered my family in the kitchen with a little cake, as we do for each of our birthdays, and I gently explained to the twins about their brother in heaven.

"He was very little in my tummy, and he went back to heaven to be with God," I said.

My son Micah looked at me and asked, "What is his name?"

For years and years there had been no name. For the longest time he had been a secret locked away deep inside me. But no longer.

"His name is Gabriel," I told Micah.

"Like the angel in my Bible?" Micah said.

"Yep," I said, kissing my son on the forehead, "just like the angel."

My time outside of that motel room with T was short, yet it profoundly touched my heart and changed me in a way that I have trouble expressing. As I hugged her good-bye, I told her I'd be praying for her, and that was a promise I kept.

Every night I prayed for T and her little son. And I joined Heidi in praying for God to whisper his name to T.

A few months later I got another text from Heidi.

"I am at the hospital. T is going into labor. Pray for her."

I waited awhile, then texted back, "How's it going?"

"Not good," Heidi answered.

At the hospital, T tested positive for drugs, something we knew was likely. Once that happened, the doctors and nurses began to treat her much differently. They were angry with her and they didn't try to hide it. Still, whether they liked it or not, T was having her baby. Heidi stayed right by her side through it all. We knew T loved her child, because you don't choose to save something you don't love. But we also knew she was numbing herself to the child's existence as a way to protect herself. The closer to the moment they got, the closer Heidi pulled toward T, continuing to love her without condemnation.

"You are not going through this alone," Heidi's actions announced. "I am here with you."

Heidi sent out prayer requests and updates throughout the day. At one point she sent a photo of a Bible sitting in her lap, opened to the first page of a book. The name "Matthew" was spelled out in big, bold text at the top of the page.

"Do you see it?" Heidi texted beneath the photo.

My eyes locked on the image on the floor of the hospital room. The overhead lights were reflecting on the white linoleum floor. The reflections intersected near the middle, forming a perfect cross.

"Don't tell me God isn't here," Heidi wrote.

I messaged her back and said, "God already knows this baby's name."

That night T had her baby.

Heidi didn't share many other details about the birth. Like I said, she is fiercely protective of her girls and their privacy. I never learned, for instance, if T got to hold her baby, or if she cried when he was born, or if his birth made her want to turn her life around. All I knew for sure was that the baby was born and given to wonderful adoptive parents.

And I know that his name is Matthew.

I thought back to the moment when I put my hand on T's belly and felt Matthew kick. It made me think of a passage in the Bible, not in Matthew, but in Luke. It is the passage about a woman who learned Jesus was in the home of a Pharisee nearby. The woman, known to everyone as a sinner, rushed in to see Jesus, and "as she stood behind Him at His feet weeping, she began to wet His feet with her tears. Then she wiped them with her hair, kissed them and poured perfume on them" (Luke 7:38).

The Pharisee condemned the woman for being a sinner, but Jesus praised her simple gesture as an act of love and an expression of humility.

To me the message of this passage is deeply powerful—we are all sinners, and we are all worthy of God's forgiveness.

That forgiveness was purchased for us by God's only Son, Jesus, on the cross, and by asking for it—by repenting—we can receive the endless blessing of God's great comfort. Some of our sins are bigger than others, and some of us are bigger sinners than others. But *all* of our sins are beyond our ability to correct. Only *God* can forgive us and redeem us and love us for who we are in spite of who we've been.

I have experienced that kind of love. When I was in heaven and I realized I was in the presence of God, I immediately surrendered to His greatness with every last shred of my being. I instantly crumpled and praised and worshipped God with all the passion I could summon. Like the woman in Luke 7:38, I hurled myself at the feet of my Creator and cried.

And what makes that moment so endlessly powerful for me—what makes me break down in tears every time I think of it—is the knowledge that, as I lay at the feet of God, He extended Himself to me. He touched me and His love engulfed me. A love that I did not deserve, but that He freely gave. *That* is the beauty of the story of the woman at the feet of Jesus. As she cries and washes His feet, the Pharisee whispers in disgust that if Jesus was Who He said He was, He'd know what kind of woman was touching Him. But Jesus *did* know.

And still—and still!—God bestows His love and forgiveness on each of us. This is why the woman wept so openly—because she, too, understood that the Lord loved her and forgave her *despite* knowing what she'd done. Her heart overflowed at the love and acceptance of her Savior.

My hand on T's belly made me think of this passage because God knows who we are and He loves us anyway. The darkness of T's life did not keep God from loving her; it only kept her from accepting that love. No one understood that more than me.

That tender fluttering under my hand as it rested on T's belly reminded me that there is no sin in the world that cannot be redeemed by God's love.

More than a year later, Heidi sent me a picture of a recent gathering she had at her home. There, in the middle of the picture, sat T. She looked good, and she was smiling and hugging Heidi. Seeing her in the photo made me smile, too.

"You can't just tell people that God loves them," Heidi once explained. "You have to do *life* with them. Then, and only then, will you have the privilege of *showing* them Who God is."

That is the essence of my journey since coming back from heaven—the journey from just telling people about God and heaven to telling *and* showing them.

In the first year of the journey, I truly struggled to give voice to the incredible *urgency* I felt to share what I had experienced in heaven. For a whole year I cried in bed every single night, because I was so frustrated at not being able to do *more* for God. That is why this book is called *Chasing Heaven* and not *Waiting Around for Heaven*—because from the very beginning I felt a call to *action*. I felt compelled to run, not walk, back to God. I felt I needed to live up to the message of James 2:17: "So you see, faith by itself isn't enough. Unless it produces good deeds, it is dead and useless" (NLT).

And so my chase began—the chase to get closer to God and to have His great love for us all shine through my life and my actions.

"Help people see You, Lord," I prayed, "through me today."

Still, I didn't know how to go about it, and I struggled mightily. Going to heaven didn't make me a Bible scholar or a Scriptures expert. I tried to be obedient when God pushed me, but sometimes I resisted. Sometimes I acted hastily and stumbled into a good deed. Sometimes I didn't do the right thing at all. But I always felt that heaven was within reach, and I learned from each action, each mistake, each leg of the chase, and over time I developed a fuller awareness of what I needed to do to help manifest God's love here on earth. I still stumble sometimes, and I still act impetuously, and Lord knows I probably always will.

My chase isn't always graceful, but it *is* always grace-filled.

What heaven taught me, and what Heidi taught me again here on earth, is that what matters most is that *we never abandon the chase*. What matters, as Heidi put it, is that we "do life" with those who need our help. It might not always be easy. It might feel downright impossible sometimes.

But even a stumble means we're moving forward—and moving closer to God.

CHAPTER TWENTY-SIX

Live Twice

I'D BEEN HELPING HEIDI WITH HER STRIP CLUB OUT-reach for about a year and a half when I started feeling another nudge. You know, one of those God nudges—the ones I usually try to ignore because most likely they'll take me out of my comfort zone, but in the end, God always wins and I end up learning something beautiful, so I'm not sure why I even fight them to begin with.

At the time, I was perfectly happy to keep tagging along with Heidi and her team. Her mission was already so established; she had built relationships with the club owners and bouncers, and of course with the girls working at the clubs, and all I had to do was show up and hand out gifts. My place on the team was important, but I didn't have the responsibility of getting donations or running the ministry. Then came the nudge, which made it clear that my work with Heidi was not supposed to be the finish line. Instead, it was just the starting point.

Very gently God let me understand He was leading me to start an outreach closer to my home. On my own.

I'd seen what an incredible commitment Heidi had made to the girls, and I understood it wasn't something I could enter into lightly. I couldn't, for instance, do it for a while and then give up. The relationships would take a long time to build. Despite my fears, I began to pray with God and asked Him to help me with the details. And as I did, I could feel Him speak to my spirit and say, "Don't worry about the details; I'll take care of them. Just step out."

I love that about God. He is so gentle and patient with someone as stubborn as me. I also love that He confirms Himself to me all the time. The same week I prayed for instructions, I received them in the form of a text message. Well, not a text from Him (though, seriously, wouldn't that be cool?) but a text from my friend Amber.

All it said was, "I think God wants us to start an outreach closer to home."

Amber is a smart, pretty mother of two who like me is married to a veteran and works as a teacher. She lives in the same little town as me and is one of the most devout Christians I've ever met. She is also probably the funniest, silliest, goofiest friend I have. When I'm around her, it is impossible not to laugh, even when nothing the least bit funny is happening. She was the perfect partner for this new adventure. So, with no road map or instructions, I said yes to God, and together Amber and I stepped out into the unknown.

There are no strip clubs in our town, so we settled on a small city about forty miles away. It was the closest place to us that had a strip club, but it also happened to be one of the most dangerous cities in America. We looked through the phone book and found the number of the club, and Amber made the call.

"Hi, we'd like to bring the girls gifts once a month," she said to the owner. "No strings attached, we just want them to know they are loved."

"No, thank you," the owner said, and hung up.

"I'm not gonna lie," Amber said, the phone still in her hand. "That didn't go like I planned it in my head."

We were off to a flying start.

We agreed to go to the club anyway, and we assembled thirty bags filled with bath lotions and body sprays tied up with pretty ribbons. On a Saturday night, we drove forty-five minutes and arrived in the town around 7:00 p.m. I knew the town fairly well; I'd graduated college there, and it had the only actual shopping mall for miles. Still, we used a GPS to find the club. Except the GPS guided us to an exit we'd never used and a part of town we'd never been to. For a while I was sure we were lost. But then, all of a sudden, we drove past a brand-new strip club that hadn't been listed in the phone book. We never would have known about it if we hadn't relied on the GPS. Now, without even discussing it, Amber and I knew we were meant to visit this club, too.

Thank you, GPS! God Positioning System, I guess you could call it.

Finally we pulled into the parking lot of the strip club we found in the phone book. We scooped up the gifts and walked to the front entrance of the club. We went up to the bouncer, a young guy in jeans and a black T-shirt with the club's name on it, and handed him a bag of homemade oatmeal-raisin cookies. He looked thoroughly confused. I'm sure it's not every night a couple of middle-aged women bring him cookies at work.

"Okay, so we're not weirdos," Amber said. "We just have some gifts we want to give to the girls."

The bouncer was no less confused, but he let us pass into the foyer of the club anyway. There, we found two stern-looking women behind a small counter. One of the women came around and stood in front of us.

"We just want to leave these for the girls," Amber told her.

The women took one of the bags and poked through it. A young blond girl standing by the counter gave us the once-over and said, "What's this for? What do y'all want?"

"We don't want anything," I said. "We just love you."

Amber and I put the gift bags on the counter. It was pretty clear the women were not going to let us pass into the club, and we didn't want to push it. We just wanted to start the relationship. We didn't know if we'd ever make it past the counter in the foyer. We were following God's plan, not our own.

"Okay, then, we'll see you next month," I said, and we smiled and walked out and back to our car.

We drove to the next club—the one we found accidentally—and dropped off a few gifts with the bartender. We never got anywhere near the girls in either club, but that was okay. We understood our progress would not be measured in days or weeks or maybe even months. Our journey was just beginning.

The next month, Amber and I assembled another round of gifts—flip-flops and nail polish this time—and drove back to the clubs. Just as we arrived at the first club, Amber began to rock back and forth.

"Oh, sweet baby Jesus," she said. "Oh, I have to go to the bathroom. My stomach is in knots."

"Do you want to try and go to the restroom in the club?" I asked her.

"Uh, no," she said. "It's okay, I'll wait."

We gave the bouncer cookies and met the same two women in the foyer. The woman who stopped us last time came around the counter and held out her hands, and we gave her the gift bags. She took them and nodded at us and walked away without a word. When we left, I wondered if the girls were even getting the gifts. But then, when we stepped outside, we saw one of the bouncers leaning against the wall eating the cookies we'd brought him.

"The girls loved the stuff you gave them last month," he told us. "And we all love the cookies."

Amber and I looked at each other and smiled.

Back in the car, as we headed to the next club, Amber told me again that she needed to go to the bathroom. It was around 11:00 p.m., and there weren't many places open in that part of town, so I kept driving and looking for a place to stop.

"I *really* need to go," Amber said as she continued rocking in her seat. "Please, God, don't let me go in Crystal's car."

"Yes, God, please don't let her do that," I added.

All I could do was speed up a little to try and find a place that was open. That's when we heard a siren and saw the bright flashing lights of a police car behind us.

"You have got to be kidding!" Amber said.

The officer came to my window, and I rolled it down.

"I'm so sorry, Officer," I said, "but I don't even know what I did wrong."

"You were going forty-six in a thirty-five," he said, looking past me at Amber, still rocking frantically in her seat.

"Officer, I'm so sorry, we're not from here," I said. "We were just trying to find a strip club."

I realized immediately that came out wrong.

"Oh?" the officer said.

"Oh, no, I mean we are just bringing gifts to the clubs," I said.

He chuckled and asked, "Exactly what kind of gift do you bring to a strip club?"

"Flip-flops and nail polish!" a squirming Amber yelled. "Flip-flops and nail polish!"

I laughed and explained her situation, and the officer let us go with a warning. A few blocks later we found a McDonald's, and I watched as Amber scurried to the restroom, grabbed the door handle, pulled, and—nothing. The door was locked.

"You have got to be *kidding* me!" she said again.

Luckily, Target was open, and Amber finally found a restroom. Afterward we made it to the second club and handed the rest of the gifts to the owner, who this time refused to let us go inside.

So, to summarize—in our first two trips for our outreach, we never got close to entering the club, almost got a speeding ticket, and Amber nearly peed in my car.

Honest to goodness, to me that truly *was* a flying start.

I often say the best day of my life was the day I died. Dying taught me so much about living. I learned not to take things for granted and to savor the moments that make up life. I learned how to stand in the light of transparency, and there is something so beautifully freeing about that. I learned that heaven is real and that there is a very real God who loves us so much.

And now I have begun to learn how to extend that love to others.

I certainly haven't learned all there is to learn on this journey. Lord knows, my life is a big old mess a lot of the time. Our twins still get daily time-outs, and I still have to send notes to their kindergarten teacher promising they will no longer hit each other or call each other "idiot." Or bark like a dog, or cut anyone's hair . . . again.

Sabyre still huffs and rolls her eyes at me when I confiscate her cell phone, and my son Payne still thinks I'm pretty lame most of the time. Even Virgil—my handsome, godly husband—still leaves his clothes all over the bathroom floor and, for the love of all things holy, can't seem to close a single kitchen cabinet door.

There are days when we're about as far from a perfect family as we can get.

Perfection, I came to learn, is an unattainable goal here on earth. I was lucky and blessed to get a tiny sampling of perfection during my minutes in heaven, and the impact of that sampling was so profound that all I've ever wanted since was the chance to experience it again. Heaven is the place we all want to get to—our ultimate destination—and I long for the day when I will be there again. I understand that heaven—not earth—is my true home.

But at the same time, I know I don't have to wait to get to heaven to feel close to God again.

What I've learned in the five years since I've been back from heaven is that our time on earth is about the journey. It is about the search, the pursuit. It is about the lessons we learn in the moments we fail, and the lessons we learn when we succeed. It's about following God even when we're scared and have no idea what we're getting into. Our journey is a journey *toward* Him, whether we're walking on the water in faith or sinking at His feet in doubt.

This is what it means to chase heaven. For Candi, the chase

led her under a bridge. For my friend Jeremy Courtney, the pursuit of heaven led him to the middle of a war zone. My friend Michelle chases heaven as she tucks the children she fosters into bed each night. Heidi's chase happens right on the streets, alongside her sisters.

For me the chase for heaven led me to all these amazing people, my friends and fellow life travelers who have each taught me so much. All of their journeys look different, but they all have one thing in common—their love for God and for the people He created.

Does this mean they are perfectly brave and fearless? Not a chance. Ask any of them and they will all tell you about the moments when they, too, began to sink in fear. But like Peter, they were close enough to the Lord for Him to grab them up before they sank. I used to be the person who stayed behind in the boat. But dying taught me how to jump out, into the water.

And as the chase continues, God will keep calling on us for more missions. We will be afraid, and we will come up short, and sometimes we'll do forty-six in a thirty-five-mile-per-hour zone. We are imperfect, every single one of us—and we are all sinners. I can promise you that when I die again I will still be a sinner. But the beautiful part is that, despite our sins and imperfections, we're still the very people the Lord wants to see jumping out of the boat and swimming toward Him.

If the stories in this book have any message at all, it is that God challenges us to find a way to put our faith into action.

For me that faith is activated through love.

When I was in heaven, God's request of me was simple—let people know I love them. That was the whole thing—God loves us. Back on earth my early thoughts were, *Really? Is that it? Nothing else?* Telling people God loves them seemed kind of boring to me. I mean, don't most people know that already—that God loves them?

And eventually God answered these doubts by saying, "Crystal, *you* didn't know it for thirty-two years."

Today, I know God's love is the most powerful weapon there is. It's the *only* weapon strong enough to change the world. It isn't boring at all—in fact, it's dangerous. God's only Son gave His *life* for this love. That love is the core of the Lord's message; it is the greatest commandment; it's the force that can end war and abuse and addiction and hunger and homelessness and bullying and so much more. Love is the weapon that takes down Satan—love defeats hate. "And now these three remain: faith, hope and love," it says in 1 Corinthians 13:13. "But the greatest of these is love."

Now here is the most wonderful part about this love—we can find it *everywhere*.

Not too long ago, the owner of a P.B. Jams restaurant in Oklahoma noticed that someone had been rooting around in the Dumpster behind her sandwich shop. So, as you might expect, the owner put up a sign near the Dumpster. It was simple and straight to the point.

"To the person going through our trash for their next meal," it read, "you're a human being and worth more than a meal from a Dumpster. Please come in during operating hours for a classic Pb&j, fresh veggies, and a cup of water at no charge. No questions asked."

She signed the message, "Your friend, the owner."

That sign is God's love in action.

That is chasing heaven.

The time I got to spend in heaven did indeed change my life, but the journey I am on today is amazing and beautiful and miraculous, and I'm so glad I got to come back to earth and take it. Heaven is in front of me, and I will forever be running toward it, and I know that one day I will get there.

But what I get to experience while I'm chasing heaven here is something I wouldn't trade for a billion dollars.

I get to find beauty in the mundane, glory in the ordinary. I get to experience God's grace in the big moments and the little ones, too. It's there on the sofa where we watch TV with a friend, and in the hospital where we tend to the sick and dying. It's in the Dumpsters and dirty alleys where the homeless sleep and in the warm bed where your child falls asleep against your chest after a nightmare. It's wrapped around the mother who kisses her baby before she places him for adoption; it's in the classroom where a teacher hugs her students; it's on the street where a police officer plays catch with the neighborhood kids.

It's in the eyes of a father as he walks his daughter down the aisle, and it's there in the broken-down prostitute, as you begin to see her as God sees her, and you realize she's just as beautiful as any pageant queen.

And it was in the tears of my friend Kelli when she learned she had lost her baby. I held her hand in the hospital and I felt God's love, too, and through those tears Kelli praised Him and told Him she loved Him anyway.

And all of these sad and wonderful moments, all of these different people who cross our paths, get woven into the gorgeous tapestry of our lives. None of it is perfect, but all of it is beautiful. And everywhere in it, we can find God's love.

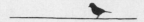

At home I tell my kids all the time that God loves them and that heaven is real. And yet I still see my children struggling from time to time to find their own relationship with God. Some days I see them get really close, but on others, I see them push God away.

"I don't know if He's real," my daughter Sabyre once said to me.

"Of course He's real!" I said. "I was with Him in heaven! I told you He is real!"

"Yeah, but that's your story, Mom," Sabyre said.

And she was right—we all have our own stories and our own journeys.

A couple of years ago the phrase "you only live once"— shortened to YOLO—became a big catchphrase in social media. Sabyre even wore a shirt with "YOLO" printed on the front.

"Gee, Mom, it's a real shame," she said to me once.

"What is?"

"That you can never wear a YOLO shirt."

We got a laugh out of that, but the idea behind it stayed with me for some time. Yes, I got to go to heaven and, in effect, live twice. But the reality is that we can *all* live twice.

We all have the opportunity to live two lives. We have the life before we knew the Lord, and the life after. The dividing line for me was heaven and the moment I surrendered everything to Him. But for others, it will be a close brush with death, or a powerful sermon, or—as it was for my husband—a simple, quiet moment when he just said yes to God.

For my dear friend Kelli, it was becoming a mom.

"I realized I couldn't do it by myself," she says. "I couldn't do it without God."

And just like that, she started her second life.

I've learned so much in the five years since those beautiful nine minutes with God, and I'm so excited to see what happens next as my chase for heaven continues.

Heaven is real, my friends. God is real. But if you take only one thing away from knowing me, please take this—God's love for you is the realest thing of all.

Acknowledgments

I AM SO BLESSED BY THE PEOPLE THAT GOD CHOSE to put into my life, many of whom made this book possible.

Virgil McVea, there are simply not enough words to describe my gratitude and love for you. You have truly been my biggest source of encouragement and I thank God daily for the gift of you in my life. The greatest day in my history was the day you caught my eye and forever changed my future. Your quiet and kind demeanor, your love for God, and your fierce love of your family are just some of the things that make you amazing. Our children are so very blessed to have you as their father, and I am blessed to be able to call you mine.

The greatest accomplishments in my life are and will always be my children. Jameson, I am so very proud of the man you are becoming. Thank you for teaching me how to love God better by loving His people better. I know that this world will be forever changed because you are a part of it. I know that mine has been. I love you, son!

Sabyre, your beauty shines from within you. Your kindness,

humor, and wit are things that make me fall more in love with you every day. I look at you and I can only imagine the plans God has for you in your life. Be bold and courageous; be fearless as you walk where He has called. Rise and rise again until the lions truly become lambs. I love you!

Micah, you are a constant source of love and joy for me. Your star definitely shines bright, my sweet boy, and I believe you will grow to accomplish everything that you dream of as a child. You are thoughtful and kind and I simply cannot get enough of your sweet kisses. I am so deeply grateful God allowed me to come back to be your mommy. I love you, my sweet boy!

Willow, my precious ray of love. You were born smiling and you have never stopped. Your little heart is so full of love for others that it makes my own heart swell. I love how you love Jesus and you remind me every day how very much Jesus loves us. I know Jesus smiles every time you end your prayers by saying, "Jesus, I hope you have a great day." I can't wait to see all that you accomplish in life. I love you so very much, baby girl.

Mom, I can never truly thank you enough for all that you have done for me. Thank you for stepping into this journey with me and for always supporting me. You have been my constant companion and I am so thankful God let you stay with me a while longer. I will never be able to adequately thank you for all of the love, time, and prayers that you have invested in me. I love you so much!

Dad, you were the first man I ever loved. I will always be thankful for our journey together, even though you had to spank me . . . once. Your work ethic and self-reliance are qualities I hope to pass on to my own children. I'm so glad you became not only my daddy but my friend.

Graham Cracker, I was determined to hate you and remind

you every day of my life that you would never replace my beloved grandma Ernie. Instead, I have spent the last thirty-one years loving you more than I ever thought possible. You are more than my grandmother; you are one of my best friends. Thank you for your humor and encouragement. I will always believe that *Waking Up in Heaven* was a bestseller because of all the time you spent in stores putting the book into people's carts.

Jayson, you are my favorite sibling by far. I'm sorry for torturing you when you were a kid by making you eat disgusting things and for always trying to scare you. (Oh, and for throwing that pool ball at your head.) Thank you for supplying my life with endless amounts of inappropriate laughter. I love you, little brother. Melissa, thanks for loving him as much as I do. I can't wait to get my signed copy of your book!

Eddie and Vernon McVea, you are two of the greatest grandparents my children could ever wish for, and the best in-laws I could have been blessed with. Thank you for always being there for us, and for loving me as if I was your own.

Sarah Spare and Kelli Baker, you are more than my best friends; you are my sisters. I am so thankful for both of you. You know that my love language is laughter, and you never cease to provide me with endless amounts of it. Thank you for sharing your hearts and your personal journeys in this book. I'm so glad that I get to do life with you two!

I am forever grateful that God led me to so many amazing people who are truly chasing heaven right here on earth. Thank you all for bravely sharing your stories within the pages of this book, and for teaching me so very much!

To Jonathan Merck, my amazing editors Ami and Katie, and to the entire Howard Books team—thank you for taking the chance on a school teacher from Oklahoma with a crazy God story that she needed desperately to share.

Nena, you are the best agent a girl could dream of having, and a precious friend. I am so blessed to have you and my Dupree Miller team! Thank you so much for continuing to support me and for always believing that the world needed this story.

Alex Tresniowski, my life was forever changed the day God brought you into it. My friendship with you is one of the greatest things this journey has brought about. Thank you for the countless hours of listening to me cry and share, for being there for me in ways this book will never depict, and for allowing me to be a part of your chase for heaven. I love you so very much, friend!